WORKERS OF ALL COUNTRIES, UNITE!

50.603

BUREAU OF ALL COUNTRIES' UNITE

毛澤東

MAO TSE-TUNG

FOUR ESSAYS ON PHILOSOPHY

FOREIGN LANGUAGES PRESS
PEKING   1968

First Edition   1966
Second Printing   1968

PUBLISHER'S NOTE

This book contains four essays on philosophy by Comrade Mao Tse-tung. "On Practice" and "On Contradiction" are included in the *Selected Works of Mao Tse-tung*, Vol. I, and "On the Correct Handling of Contradictions Among the People" and "Where Do Correct Ideas Come from?" in *Articles and Extracts from the Works of Mao Tse-tung (Selection A)*. The notes have been rearranged and partly revised by the Committee for the Publication of the Selected Works of Mao Tse-tung with a view to the needs of readers abroad.

Printed in the People's Republic of China

CONTENTS

CONTENTS

ON PRACTICE

On the Relation Between Knowledge and Practice,
Between Knowing and Doing

July 1937

Before Marx, materialism examined the problem of knowledge apart from the social nature of man and apart from his historical development, and was therefore incapable of understanding the dependence of knowledge on social practice, that is, the dependence of knowledge on production and the class struggle.

Above all, Marxists regard man's activity in production as the most fundamental practical activity, the determinant of all his other activities. Man's knowledge depends mainly on his activity in material production, through which he comes gradually to understand the phenomena, the properties and the laws of nature, and the relations between himself and

There used to be a number of comrades in our Party who were dogmatists and who for a long period rejected the experience of the Chinese revolution, denying the truth that "Marxism is not a dogma but a guide to action" and overawing people with words and phrases from Marxist works, torn out of context. There were also a number of comrades who were empiricists and who for a long period restricted themselves to their own fragmentary experience and did not understand the importance of theory for revolutionary practice or see the revolution as a whole, but worked blindly though industriously. The erroneous ideas of these two types of comrades, and particularly of the dogmatists, nature; and through his activity in production he also gradually comes to understand, in varying degrees, certain relations that exist between man and man. None of this knowledge can be acquired apart from activity in production. In a classless society every person, as a member of society, joins in common effort with the other members, enters into definite relations of production with them and engages in production to meet man's material needs. In all class societies, the members of the different social classes also enter, in different ways, into definite relations of production and engage in production to meet their material needs. This is the primary source from which human knowledge develops.

Man's social practice is not confined to activity in production, but takes many other forms — class struggle, political life, scientific and artistic pursuits; in short, as a social being, man participates in all spheres of the practical life of society. Thus man, in varying degrees, comes to know the different relations between man and man, not only through his material life but also through his political and cultural life (both of which are intimately bound up with material life). Of these other types of social practice, class struggle in particular, in all its various forms, exerts a profound influence on the development of man's knowledge. In class society everyone lives as a member of a particular class, and every kind of

caused enormous losses to the Chinese revolution during 1931-34, and yet the dogmatists, cloaking themselves as Marxists, confused a great many comrades. "On Practice" was written in order to expose the subjectivist errors of dogmatism and empiricism in the Party, and especially the error of dogmatism, from the standpoint of the Marxist theory of knowledge. It was entitled "On Practice" because its stress was on exposing the dogmatist kind of subjectivism, which belittles practice. The ideas contained in this essay were presented by Comrade Mao Tse-tung in a lecture at the Anti-Japanese Military and Political College in Yenan.

thinking, without exception, is stamped with the brand of a class.

Marxists hold that in human society activity in production develops step by step from a lower to a higher level and that consequently man's knowledge, whether of nature or of society, also develops step by step from a lower to a higher level, that is, from the shallower to the deeper, from the one-sided to the many-sided. For a very long period in history, men were necessarily confined to a one-sided understanding of the history of society because, for one thing, the bias of the exploiting classes always distorted history and, for another, the small scale of production limited man's outlook. It was not until the modern proletariat emerged along with immense forces of production (large-scale industry) that man was able to acquire a comprehensive, historical understanding of the development of society and turn this knowledge into a science, the science of Marxism.

Marxists hold that man's social practice alone is the criterion of the truth of his knowledge of the external world. What actually happens is that man's knowledge is verified only when he achieves the anticipated results in the process of social practice (material production, class struggle or scientific experiment). If a man wants to succeed in his work, that is, to achieve the anticipated results, he must bring his ideas into correspondence with the laws of the objective external world; if they do not correspond, he will fail in his practice. After he fails, he draws his lessons, corrects his ideas to make them correspond to the laws of the external world, and can thus turn failure into success; this is what is meant by "failure is the mother of success" and "a fall into the pit, a gain in your wit". The dialectical-materialist theory of knowledge places practice in the primary position, holding that human knowledge can in no way be separated from practice and repudiating all the erroneous theories which deny the importance of practice or separate knowledge from practice. Thus Lenin said, "*Practice is higher than (theoretical) knowledge*, for it has not only the dignity of universality, but also of immediate actuality."[1] The Marxist philosophy of dialectical materialism has two outstanding characteristics. One is its class nature: it openly avows that dialectical materialism is in the service of the proletariat. The other is its practicality: it emphasizes the dependence of theory on practice, emphasizes that theory is based on practice and in turn serves practice. The truth of any knowledge or theory is determined not by subjective feelings, but by objective results in social practice. Only social practice can be the criterion of truth. The standpoint of practice is the primary and basic standpoint in the dialectical-materialist theory of knowledge.[2]

But how then does human knowledge arise from practice and in turn serve practice? This will become clear if we look at the process of development of knowledge.

In the process of practice, man at first sees only the phenomenal side, the separate aspects, the external relations of things. For instance, some people from outside come to Yenan on a tour of observation. In the first day or two, they see its topography, streets and houses; they meet many people, attend banquets, evening parties and mass meetings, hear talk of various kinds and read various documents, all these being the phenomena, the separate aspects and the external relations of things. This is called the perceptual stage of cognition, namely, the stage of sense perceptions and impressions. That is, these particular things in Yenan act on the sense organs of the members of the observation group, evoke

4

sense perceptions and give rise in their brains to many impressions together with a rough sketch of the external relations among these impressions: this is the first stage of cognition. At this stage, man cannot as yet form concepts, which are deeper, or draw logical conclusions.

As social practice continues, things that give rise to man's sense perceptions and impressions in the course of his practice are repeated many times; then a sudden change (leap) takes place in the brain in the process of cognition, and concepts are formed. Concepts are no longer the phenomena, the separate aspects and the external relations of things; they grasp the essence, the totality and the internal relations of things. Between concepts and sense perceptions there is not only a quantitative but also a qualitative difference. Proceeding further, by means of judgement and inference one is able to draw logical conclusions. The expression in *San Kuo Yen Yi*,[3] "knit the brows and a stratagem comes to mind", or in everyday language, "let me think it over", refers to man's use of concepts in the brain to form judgements and inferences. This is the second stage of cognition. When the members of the observation group have collected various data and, what is more, have "thought them over", they are able to arrive at the judgement that "the Communist Party's policy of the National United Front Against Japan is thorough, sincere and genuine". Having made this judgement, they can, if they too are genuine about uniting to save the nation, go a step further and draw the following conclusion, "The National United Front Against Japan can succeed." This stage of conception, judgement and inference is the more important stage in the entire process of knowing a thing; it is the stage of rational knowledge. The real task of knowing is, through perception, to arrive at thought, to arrive step by step at the comprehension of the internal contradictions of objective things, of their laws and of the internal relations between one process and another, that is, to arrive at logical knowledge. To repeat, logical knowledge differs from perceptual knowledge in that perceptual knowledge pertains to the separate aspects, the phenomena and the external relations of things, whereas logical knowledge takes a big stride forward to reach the totality, the essence and the internal relations of things and discloses the inner contradictions in the surrounding world. Therefore, logical knowledge is capable of grasping the development of the surrounding world in its totality, in the internal relations of all its aspects.

This dialectical-materialist theory of the process of development of knowledge, basing itself on practice and proceeding from the shallower to the deeper, was never worked out by anybody before the rise of Marxism. Marxist materialism solved this problem correctly for the first time, pointing out both materialistically and dialectically the deepening movement of cognition, the movement by which man in society progresses from perceptual knowledge to logical knowledge in his complex, constantly recurring practice of production and class struggle. Lenin said, "The abstraction of *matter,* of a *law* of nature, the abstraction of *value,* etc., in short, *all* scientific (correct, serious, not absurd) abstractions reflect nature more deeply, truly and *completely.*"[4] Marxism-Leninism holds that each of the two stages in the process of cognition has its own characteristics, with knowledge manifesting itself as perceptual at the lower stage and logical at the higher stage, but that both are stages in an integrated process of cognition. The perceptual and the rational are qualitatively different, but are not divorced from each other; they are unified on the basis of practice. Our practice proves that what is perceived

6

cannot at once be comprehended and that only what is comprehended can be more deeply perceived. Perception only solves the problem of phenomena; theory alone can solve the problem of essence. The solving of both these problems is not separable in the slightest degree from practice. Whoever wants to know a thing has no way of doing so except by coming into contact with it, that is, by living (practising) in its environment. In feudal society it was impossible to know the laws of capitalist society in advance because capitalism had not yet emerged, the relevant practice was lacking. Marxism could be the product only of capitalist society. Marx, in the era of laissez-faire capitalism, could not concretely know certain laws peculiar to the era of imperialism beforehand, because imperialism, the last stage of capitalism, had not yet emerged and the relevant practice was lacking; only Lenin and Stalin could undertake this task. Leaving aside their genius, the reason why Marx, Engels, Lenin and Stalin could work out their theories was mainly that they personally took part in the practice of the class struggle and the scientific experimentation of their time; lacking this condition, no genius could have succeeded. The saying, "without stepping outside his gate the scholar knows all the wide world's affairs", was mere empty talk in past times when technology was undeveloped. Even though this saying can be valid in the present age of developed technology, the people with real personal knowledge are those engaged in practice the wide world over. And it is only when these people have come to "know" through their practice and when their knowledge has reached him through writing and technical media that the "scholar" can indirectly "know all the wide world's affairs". If you want to know a certain thing or a certain class of things directly, you must personally partici-

7

pate in the practical struggle to change reality, to change that thing or class of things, for only thus can you come into contact with them as phenomena; only through personal participation in the practical struggle to change reality can you uncover the essence of that thing or class of things and comprehend them. This is the path to knowledge which every man actually travels, though some people, deliberately distorting matters, argue to the contrary. The most ridiculous person in the world is the "know-all" who picks up a smattering of hearsay knowledge and proclaims himself "the world's Number One authority"; this merely shows that he has not taken a proper measure of himself. Knowledge is a matter of science, and no dishonesty or conceit whatsoever is permissible. What is required is definitely the reverse — honesty and modesty. If you want knowledge, you must take part in the practice of changing reality. If you want to know the taste of a pear, you must change the pear by eating it yourself. If you want to know the structure and properties of the atom, you must make physical and chemical experiments to change the state of the atom. If you want to know the theory and methods of revolution, you must take part in revolution. All genuine knowledge originates in direct experience. But one cannot have direct experience of everything; as a matter of fact, most of our knowledge comes from indirect experience, for example, all knowledge from past times and foreign lands. To our ancestors and to foreigners, such knowledge was — or is — a matter of direct experience, and this knowledge is reliable if in the course of their direct experience the requirement of "scientific abstraction", spoken of by Lenin, was — or is — fulfilled and objective reality scientifically reflected; otherwise it is not reliable. Hence a man's knowledge consists only of two parts, that which comes from direct experience and that which comes from indirect experience. Moreover, what is indirect experience for me is direct experience for other people. Consequently, considered as a whole, knowledge of any kind is inseparable from direct experience. All knowledge originates in perception of the objective external world through man's physical sense organs. Anyone who denies such perception, denies direct experience, or denies personal participation in the practice that changes reality, is not a materialist. That is why the "know-all" is ridiculous. There is an old Chinese saying, "How can you catch tiger cubs without entering the tiger's lair?" This saying holds true for man's practice and it also holds true for the theory of knowledge. There can be no knowledge apart from practice.

To make clear the dialectical-materialist movement of cognition arising on the basis of the practice which changes reality — to make clear the gradually deepening movement of cognition — a few additional concrete examples are given below.

In its knowledge of capitalist society, the proletariat was only in the perceptual stage of cognition in the first period of its practice, the period of machine-smashing and spontaneous struggle; it knew only some of the aspects and the external relations of the phenomena of capitalism. The proletariat was then still a "class-in-itself". But when it reached the second period of its practice, the period of conscious and organized economic and political struggles, the proletariat was able to comprehend the essence of capitalist society, the relations of exploitation between social classes and its own historical task; and it was able to do so because of its own practice and because of its experience of prolonged struggle, which Marx and Engels scientifically summed up in all its variety to create the theory of Marxism for the education of the proletariat. It was then that the proletariat became a "class-for-itself".

Similarly with the Chinese people's knowledge of imperialism. The first stage was one of superficial, perceptual knowledge, as shown in the indiscriminate anti-foreign struggles of the Movement of the Taiping Heavenly Kingdom,[5] the Yi Ho Tuan Movement,[6] and so on. It was only in the second stage that the Chinese people reached the stage of rational knowledge, saw the internal and external contradictions of imperialism and saw the essential truth that imperialism had allied itself with China's comprador and feudal classes to oppress and exploit the great masses of the Chinese people. This knowledge began about the time of the May 4th Movement of 1919.[7]

Next, let us consider war. If those who lead a war lack experience of war, then at the initial stage they will not understand the profound laws pertaining to the directing of a specific war (such as our Agrarian Revolutionary War of the past decade). At the initial stage they will merely experience a good deal of fighting and, what is more, suffer many defeats. But this experience (the experience of battles won and especially of battles lost) enables them to comprehend the inner thread of the whole war, namely, the laws of that specific war, to understand its strategy and tactics, and consequently to direct the war with confidence. If, at such a moment, the command is turned over to an inexperienced person, then he too will have to suffer a number of defeats (gain experience) before he can comprehend the true laws of the war.

"I am not sure I can handle it." We often hear this remark when a comrade hesitates to accept an assignment. Why is he unsure of himself? Because he has no systematic understanding of the content and circumstances of the assignment, or because he has had little or no contact with such work, and so the laws governing it are beyond him. After a detailed analysis of the nature and circumstances of the assignment, he will feel more sure of himself and do it willingly. If he spends some time at the job and gains experience and if he is a person who is willing to look into matters with an open mind and not one who approaches problems subjectively, one-sidedly and superficially, then he can draw conclusions for himself as to how to go about the job and do it with much more courage. Only those who are subjective, one-sided and superficial in their approach to problems will smugly issue orders or directives the moment they arrive on the scene, without considering the circumstances, without viewing things in their totality (their history and their present state as a whole) and without getting to the essence of things (their nature and the internal relations between one thing and another). Such people are bound to trip and fall.

Thus it can be seen that the first step in the process of cognition is contact with the objects of the external world; this belongs to the stage of perception. The second step is to synthesize the data of perception by arranging and reconstructing them; this belongs to the stage of conception, judgement and inference. It is only when the data of perception are very rich (not fragmentary) and correspond to reality (are not illusory) that they can be the basis for forming correct concepts and theories.

Here two important points must be emphasized. The first, which has been stated before but should be repeated here, is the dependence of rational knowledge upon perceptual knowledge. Anyone who thinks that rational knowledge need not be derived from perceptual knowledge is an idealist. In the history of philosophy there is the "rationalist" school that admits the reality only of reason and not of experience, believing that reason alone is reliable while perceptual experience is not; this school errs by turning things upside down. The rational is reliable precisely because it has its source in sense perceptions, otherwise it would be like water without a source, a tree without roots, subjective, self-engendered and unreliable. As to the sequence in the process of cognition, perceptual experience comes first; we stress the significance of social practice in the process of cognition precisely because social practice alone can give rise to human knowledge and it alone can start man on the acquisition of perceptual experience from the objective world. For a person who shuts his eyes, stops his ears and totally cuts himself off from the objective world there can be no such thing as knowledge. Knowledge begins with experience — this is the materialism of the theory of knowledge.

The second point is that knowledge needs to be deepened, that the perceptual stage of knowledge needs to be developed to the rational stage — this is the dialectics of the theory of knowledge.[8] To think that knowledge can stop at the lower, perceptual stage and that perceptual knowledge alone is reliable while rational knowledge is not, would be to repeat the historical error of "empiricism". This theory errs in failing to understand that, although the data of perception reflect certain realities in the objective world (I am not speaking here of idealist empiricism which confines experience to so-called introspection), they are merely one-sided and superficial, reflecting things incompletely and not reflecting their essence. Fully to reflect a thing in its totality, to reflect its essence, to reflect its inherent laws, it is necessary through the exercise of thought to reconstruct the rich data of sense perception, discarding the dross and selecting the essential, eliminating the false and retaining the true, proceeding from the one to the other and from the outside to the inside, in order to form a system of concepts and theories — it is necessary to make a leap from perceptual to rational knowledge. Such reconstructed knowledge is not more empty or more unreliable; on the contrary, whatever has been scientifically reconstructed in the process of cognition, on the basis of practice, reflects objective reality, as Lenin said, more deeply, more truly, more fully. As against this, vulgar "practical men" respect experience but despise theory, and therefore cannot have a comprehensive view of an entire objective process, lack clear direction and long-range perspective, and are complacent over occasional successes and glimpses of the truth. If such persons direct a revolution, they will lead it up a blind alley.

Rational knowledge depends upon perceptual knowledge and perceptual knowledge remains to be developed into rational knowledge — this is the dialectical-materialist theory of knowledge. In philosophy, neither "rationalism" nor "empiricism" understands the historical or the dialectical nature of knowledge, and although each of these schools contains one aspect of the truth (here I am referring to materialist, not to idealist, rationalism and empiricism), both are wrong on the theory of knowledge as a whole. The dialectical-materialist movement of knowledge from the perceptual to the rational holds true for a minor process of cognition (for instance, knowing a single thing or task) as well as for a major process of cognition (for instance, knowing a whole society or a revolution).

But the movement of knowledge does not end here. If the dialectical-materialist movement of knowledge were to stop at rational knowledge, only half the problem would be dealt with. And as far as Marxist philosophy is concerned, only the less important half at that. Marxist philosophy holds that the most important problem does not lie in understanding the laws of the objective world and thus being able to explain it, but in applying the knowledge of these laws actively to change the world. From the Marxist viewpoint, theory is important, and its importance is fully expressed in Lenin's statement, "Without revolutionary theory there can be no revolutionary movement."[9] But Marxism emphasizes the importance of theory precisely and only because it can guide action. If we have a correct theory but merely prate about it, pigeonhole it and do not put it into practice, then that theory, however good, is of no significance. Knowledge begins with practice, and theoretical knowledge is acquired through practice and must then return to practice. The active function of knowledge manifests itself not only in the active leap from perceptual to rational knowledge, but — and this is more important — it must manifest itself in the leap from rational knowledge to revolutionary practice. The knowledge which grasps the laws of the world, must be redirected to the practice of changing the world, must be applied anew in the practice of production, in the practice of revolutionary class struggle and revolutionary national struggle and in the practice of scientific experiment. This is the process of testing and developing theory, the continuation of the whole process of cognition. The problem of whether theory corresponds to objective reality is not, and cannot be, completely solved in the movement of knowledge from the perceptual to the rational, mentioned above. The only way to solve this problem completely is to redirect rational knowledge to social practice, apply theory to practice and see whether it can achieve the objectives one has in mind. Many theories of natural science are held to be true not only because they were so considered when natural scientists originated them, but because they have been verified in subsequent scientific practice. Similarly, Marxism-Leninism is held to be true not only because it was so considered when it was scientifically formulated by Marx, Engels, Lenin and Stalin but because it has been verified in the subsequent practice of revolutionary class struggle and revolutionary national struggle. Dialectical materialism is universally true because it is impossible for anyone to escape from its domain in his practice. The history of human knowledge tells us that the truth of many theories is incomplete and that this incompleteness is remedied through the test of practice. Many theories are erroneous and it is through the test of practice that their errors are corrected. That is why practice is the criterion of truth and why "the standpoint of life, of practice, should be first and fundamental in the theory of knowledge".[10] Stalin has well said, "Theory becomes purposeless if it is not connected with revolutionary practice, just as practice gropes in the dark if its path is not illumined by revolutionary theory."[11]

When we get to this point, is the movement of knowledge completed? Our answer is: it is and yet it is not. When men in society throw themselves into the practice of changing a certain objective process (whether natural or social) at a certain stage of its development, they can, as a result of the reflection of the objective process in their brains and the exercise of their conscious dynamic role, advance their knowledge from the perceptual to the rational, and create ideas, theories, plans or programmes which correspond in general to the laws of that objective process. They then apply these ideas, theories, plans or programmes in practice in the same objective process. And if they can realize the aims they have in mind, that is, if in that same process of practice they can translate, or on the whole translate, those previously formulated ideas, theories, plans or programmes into fact, then the movement of knowledge may be considered completed with regard to this particular process. In the process of changing nature, take for example the fulfilment of an engineering plan, the verification of a scientific hypothesis, the manufacture of an implement or the reaping of a crop; or in the process of changing society, take for example the victory of a strike, victory in a war or the fulfilment of an educational plan. All these may be considered the realization of aims one has in mind. But generally speaking, whether in the practice of changing nature or of changing society, men's original ideas, theories, plans or programmes are seldom realized without any alteration. This is because people engaged in changing reality are usually subject to numerous limitations; they are limited not only by existing scientific and technological conditions but also by the development of the objective process itself and the degree to which this process has become manifest (the aspects and the essence of the objective process have not yet been fully revealed). In such a situation, ideas, theories, plans or programmes are usually altered partially and sometimes even wholly, because of the discovery of unforeseen circumstances in the course of practice. That is to say, it does happen that the original ideas, theories, plans or programmes fail to correspond with reality either in whole or in part and are wholly or partially incorrect. In many instances, failures have to be repeated many times before errors in knowledge can be corrected and correspondence with the laws of the objective process achieved, and consequently before the subjective can be transformed into the objective, or in other words, before the anticipated results can be achieved in practice. Nevertheless, when that point is reached, the movement of human knowledge regarding a certain objective process at a certain stage of its development may be considered completed.

However, so far as the progression of the process is concerned, the movement of human knowledge is not completed. Every process, whether in the realm of nature or of society, progresses and develops by reason of its internal contradiction and struggle, and the movement of human knowledge should also progress and develop along with it. As far as social movements are concerned, true revolutionary leaders must not only be good at correcting their ideas, theories, plans or programmes when errors are discovered, as has been indicated above; but when a certain objective process has already progressed and changed from one stage of development to another, they must also be good at making themselves and all their fellow-revolutionaries progress and change in their subjective knowledge along with it, that is to say, they must ensure that the proposed new revolutionary tasks and new working programmes correspond to the new changes in the situation. In a revolutionary period the situation changes very rapidly; if the knowledge of revolutionaries does not change rapidly in accordance with the changed situation, they will be unable to lead the revolution to victory.

It often happens, however, that thinking lags behind reality; this is because man's cognition is limited by numerous social conditions. We are opposed to die-hards in the revolutionary ranks whose thinking fails to advance with changing objective circumstances and has manifested itself historically as Right opportunism. These people fail to see that the struggle of opposites has already pushed the objective process forward while their knowledge has stopped at the old stage. This is characteristic of the thinking of all die-hards. Their thinking is divorced from social practice, and they cannot march ahead to guide the chariot of society; they simply trail behind, grumbling that it goes too fast and trying to drag it back or turn it in the opposite direction.

We are also opposed to "Left" phrase-mongering. The thinking of "Leftists" outstrips a given stage of development of the objective process; some regard their fantasies as truth, while others strain to realize in the present an ideal which can only be realized in the future. They alienate themselves from the current practice of the majority of the people and from the realities of the day, and show themselves adventurist in their actions.

Idealism and mechanical materialism, opportunism and adventurism, are all characterized by the breach between the subjective and the objective, by the separation of knowledge from practice. The Marxist-Leninist theory of knowledge, characterized as it is by scientific social practice, cannot but resolutely oppose these wrong ideologies. Marxists recognize that in the absolute and general process of development of the universe, the development of each particular process is relative, and that hence, in the endless flow of absolute truth, man's knowledge of a particular process at any given stage of development is only relative truth. The sum total of innumerable relative truths constitutes absolute truth.[12] The development of an objective process is full of contradictions and struggles, and so is the development of the movement of human knowledge. All the dialectical movements of the objective world can sooner or later be reflected in human knowledge. In social practice, the process of coming into being, developing and passing away is infinite, and so is the process of coming into being, developing and passing away in human knowledge. As man's practice which changes objective reality in accordance with given ideas, theories, plans or programmes, advances further and further, his knowledge of objective reality likewise becomes deeper and deeper. The movement of change in the world of objective reality is never-ending and so is man's cognition of truth through practice. Marxism-Leninism has in no way exhausted truth but ceaselessly opens up roads to the knowledge of truth in the course of practice. Our conclusion is the concrete, historical unity of the subjective and the objective, of theory and practice, of knowing and doing, and we are opposed to all erroneous ideologies, whether "Left" or Right, which depart from concrete history.

In the present epoch of the development of society, the responsibility of correctly knowing and changing the world has been placed by history upon the shoulders of the proletariat and its party. This process, the practice of changing the world, which is determined in accordance with scientific knowledge, has already reached a historic moment in the world and in China, a great moment unprecedented in human history, that is, the moment for completely banishing darkness from the world and from China and for changing the world into a world of light such as never previously existed. The struggle of the proletariat and the revolutionary people to change the world comprises the fulfilment of the following tasks: to change the objective world and, at the same time, their own subjective world — to change their cognitive ability and change the relations between the subjective and the objective world. Such a change has already come about in one part of the globe, in the Soviet Union. There the people are pushing forward this process of change. The people of China and the rest of the world either are going through, or will go through, such a process. And the objective world which is to be changed also includes all the opponents of change, who, in order to be changed, must go through a stage of compulsion before they can enter the stage of voluntary, conscious change. The epoch of world communism will be reached when all mankind voluntarily and consciously changes itself and the world.

Discover the truth through practice, and again through practice verify and develop the truth. Start from perceptual knowledge and actively develop it into rational knowledge; then start from rational knowledge and actively guide revolutionary practice to change both the subjective and the objective world. Practice, knowledge, again practice, and again knowledge. This form repeats itself in endless cycles, and with each cycle the content of practice and knowledge rises to a higher level. Such is the whole of the dialectical-materialist theory of knowledge, and such is the dialectical-materialist theory of the unity of knowing and doing.

NOTES

[1] From Lenin's notes on "The Idea" in Hegel's *The Science of Logic*, Book III, Section 3. See V. I. Lenin, "Conspectus of Hegel's *The Science of Logic*" (September-December 1914), *Collected Works*, Russ. ed., Moscow, 1958, Vol. XXXVIII, p. 205.

[2] See Karl Marx, "Theses on Feuerbach" (spring of 1845), Karl Marx and Frederick Engels, *Selected Works*, in two volumes, Eng. ed., FLPH, Moscow, 1958, Vol. II, p. 403, and V. I. Lenin, *Materialism and Empirio-Criticism* (second half of 1908), Eng. ed., FLPH, Moscow, 1952, pp. 136-42.

[3] *San Kuo Yen Yi (Tales of the Three Kingdoms)* is a famous Chinese historical novel by Lo Kuan-chung (late 14th and early 15th century).

[4] From Lenin's notes on "Subjective Logic or the Doctrine of the Notion" in Hegel's *The Science of Logic*, Book III. See V. I. Lenin, "Conspectus of Hegel's *The Science of Logic*", *Collected Works*, Russ. ed., Moscow, 1958, Vol. XXXVIII, p. 161.

[5] The Movement of the Taiping Heavenly Kingdom was the mid-19th century revolutionary peasant war against the feudal rule and national oppression of the Ching Dynasty. In January 1851 Hung Hsiu-chuan, Yang Hsiu-ching and other leaders launched an uprising in Chintien Village in Kueiping County, Kwangsi Province, and proclaimed the founding of the Taiping Heavenly Kingdom. Proceeding northward from Kwangsi, their peasant army attacked and occupied Hunan and Hupeh in 1852. In 1853 it marched through Kiangsi and Anhwei and captured Nanking. A section of the forces then continued the drive north and pushed on to the vicinity of Tientsin. However, the Taiping army failed to build stable base areas in the places it occupied; moreover, after establishing its capital in Nanking, its leading group committed many political and military errors. Therefore it was unable to withstand the combined onslaughts of the counter-revolutionary forces of the Ching government and the British, U.S. and French aggressors, and was finally defeated in 1864.

[6] The Yi Ho Tuan Movement was the anti-imperialist armed struggle which took place in northern China in 1900. The broad masses of peasants, handicraftsmen and other people took part in this movement. Getting in touch with one another through religious and other channels, they organized themselves on the basis of secret societies and waged a heroic struggle against the joint forces of aggression of the eight imperialist powers — the United States, Britain, Japan, Germany, Russia, France, Italy and Austria. The movement was put down with indescribable savagery after the joint forces of aggression occupied Tientsin and Peking.

[7] The May 4th Movement was an anti-imperialist and anti-feudal revolutionary movement which began on May 4, 1919. In the first half of that year, the victors of World War I, *i.e.*, Britain, France, the United

States, Japan, Italy and other imperialist countries, met in Paris to divide the spoils and decided that Japan should take over all the privileges previously enjoyed by Germany in Shantung Province, China. The students of Peking were the first to show determined opposition to this scheme, holding rallies and demonstrations on May 4. The Northern warlord government arrested more than thirty students in an effort to suppress this opposition. In protest, the students of Peking went on strike and large numbers of students in other parts of the country responded. On June 3 the Northern warlord government started arresting students in Peking en masse, and within two days about a thousand were taken into custody. This aroused still greater indignation throughout the country. From June 5 onwards, the workers of Shanghai and many other cities went on strike and the merchants in these places shut their shops. Thus, what was at first a patriotic movement consisting mainly of intellectuals rapidly developed into a national patriotic movement embracing the proletariat, the urban petty bourgeoisie and the bourgeoisie. And along with the growth of this patriotic movement, the new cultural movement which had begun before May 4 as a movement against feudalism and for the promotion of science and democracy, grew into a vigorous and powerful revolutionary cultural movement whose main current was the propagation of Marxism-Leninism.

[8] See Lenin's notes on "The Idea" in Hegel's *The Science of Logic*, Book III, Section 3, in which he said: "In order to understand, it is necessary empirically to begin understanding, study, to rise from empiricism to the universal." (V. I. Lenin, "Conspectus of Hegel's *The Science of Logic*", *Collected Works*, Russ. ed., Moscow, 1958, Vol. XXXVIII, p. 197.)

[9] V. I. Lenin, "What Is to Be Done?" (autumn 1901-February 1902), *Collected Works*, Eng. ed., FLPH, Moscow, 1961, Vol. V, p. 369.

[10] V. I. Lenin, *Materialism and Empirio-Criticism*, Eng. ed., FLPH, Moscow, 1952, p. 141.

[11] J. V. Stalin, "The Foundations of Leninism" (April-May 1924), *Problems of Leninism*, Eng. ed., FLPH, Moscow, 1954, p. 31.

[12] See V. I. Lenin, *Materialism and Empirio-Criticism*, Eng. ed., FLPH, Moscow, 1952, pp. 129-36.

ON CONTRADICTION

August 1937

The law of contradiction in things, that is, the law of the unity of opposites, is the basic law of materialist dialectics. Lenin said, "Dialectics in the proper sense is the study of contradiction *in the very essence of objects*."[1] Lenin often called this law the essence of dialectics; he also called it the kernel of dialectics.[2] In studying this law, therefore, we cannot but touch upon a variety of questions, upon a number of philosophical problems. If we can become clear on all these problems, we shall arrive at a fundamental understanding of materialist dialectics. The problems are: the two world outlooks, the universality of contradiction, the particularity of contradiction, the principal contradiction and the principal aspect of a contradiction, the identity and struggle of the aspects of a contradiction, and the place of antagonism in contradiction.

The criticism to which the idealism of the Deborin school[3] has been subjected in Soviet philosophical circles in recent years has aroused great interest among us. Deborin's ideal-

---

This essay on philosophy was written by Comrade Mao Tse-tung after his essay "On Practice" and with the same object of overcoming the serious error of dogmatist thinking to be found in the Party at the time. Originally delivered as lectures at the Anti-Japanese Military and Political College in Yenan, it was revised by the author on its inclusion in his *Selected Works*.

ism has exerted a very bad influence in the Chinese Communist Party, and it cannot be said that the dogmatist thinking in our Party is unrelated to the approach of that school. Our present study of philosophy should therefore have the eradication of dogmatist thinking as its main objective.

I. THE TWO WORLD OUTLOOKS

Throughout the history of human knowledge, there have been two conceptions concerning the law of development of the universe, the metaphysical conception and the dialectical conception, which form two opposing world outlooks. Lenin said:

> The two basic (or two possible? or two historically observable?) conceptions of development (evolution) are: development as decrease and increase, as repetition, *and* development as a unity of opposites (the division of a unity into mutually exclusive opposites and their reciprocal relation).[4]

Here Lenin was referring to these two different world outlooks.

In China another name for metaphysics is *hsuan-hsueh*. For a long period in history whether in China or in Europe, this way of thinking, which is part and parcel of the idealist world outlook, occupied a dominant position in human thought. In Europe, the materialism of the bourgeoisie in its early days was also metaphysical. As the social economy of many European countries advanced to the stage of highly developed capitalism, as the forces of production, the class struggle and the sciences developed to a level unprecedented

24

in history, and as the industrial proletariat became the greatest motive force in historical development, there arose the Marxist world outlook of materialist dialectics. Then, in addition to open and barefaced reactionary idealism, vulgar evolutionism emerged among the bourgeoisie to oppose materialist dialectics.

The metaphysical or vulgar evolutionist world outlook sees things as isolated, static and one-sided. It regards all things in the universe, their forms and their species, as eternally isolated from one another and immutable. Such change as there is can only be an increase or decrease in quantity or a change of place. Moreover, the cause of such an increase or decrease or change of place is not inside things but outside them, that is, the motive force is external. Metaphysicians hold that all the different kinds of things in the universe and all their characteristics have been the same ever since they first came into being. All subsequent changes have simply been increases or decreases in quantity. They contend that a thing can only keep on repeating itself as the same kind of thing and cannot change into anything different. In their opinion, capitalist exploitation, capitalist competition, the individualist ideology of capitalist society, and so on, can all be found in ancient slave society, or even in primitive society, and will exist for ever unchanged. They ascribe the causes of social development to factors external to society, such as geography and climate. They search in an over-simplified way outside a thing for the causes of its development, and they deny the theory of materialist dialectics which holds that development arises from the contradictions inside a thing. Consequently they can explain neither the qualitative diversity of things, nor the phenomenon of one quality changing into another. In Europe, this mode of thinking existed as mechanical materialism in the 17th and 18th centuries and as vulgar evolutionism at the end of the 19th and the beginning of the 20th centuries. In China, there was the metaphysical thinking exemplified in the saying "Heaven changeth not, likewise the Tao changeth not",[5] and it was supported by the decadent feudal ruling classes for a long time. Mechanical materialism and vulgar evolutionism, which were imported from Europe in the last hundred years, are supported by the bourgeoisie.

As opposed to the metaphysical world outlook, the world outlook of materialist dialectics holds that in order to understand the development of a thing we should study it internally and in its relations with other things; in other words, the development of things should be seen as their internal and necessary self-movement, while each thing in its movement is interrelated with and interacts on the things around it. The fundamental cause of the development of a thing is not external but internal; it lies in the contradictoriness within the thing. There is internal contradiction in every single thing, hence its motion and development. Contradictoriness within a thing is the fundamental cause of its development, while its interrelations and interactions with other things are secondary causes. Thus materialist dialectics effectively combats the theory of external causes, or of an external motive force, advanced by metaphysical mechanical materialism and vulgar evolutionism. It is evident that purely external causes can only give rise to mechanical motion, that is, to changes in scale or quantity, but cannot explain why things differ qualitatively in thousands of ways and why one thing changes into another. As a matter of fact, even mechanical motion under external force occurs through the internal contradictoriness of things. Simple growth in plants and animals, their quantitative development, is likewise chiefly the result of their internal contradictions. Similarly, social development is due chiefly not to external but to internal causes. Countries with almost the same geographical and climatic conditions display great diversity and unevenness in their development. Moreover, great social changes may take place in one and the same country although its geography and climate remain unchanged. Imperialist Russia changed into the socialist Soviet Union, and feudal Japan, which had locked its doors against the world, changed into imperialist Japan, although no change occurred in the geography and climate of either country. Long dominated by feudalism, China has undergone great changes in the last hundred years and is now changing in the direction of a new China, liberated and free, and yet no change has occurred in her geography and climate. Changes do take place in the geography and climate of the earth as a whole and in every part of it, but they are insignificant when compared with changes in society; geographical and climatic changes manifest themselves in terms of tens of thousands of years, while social changes manifest themselves in thousands, hundreds or tens of years, and even in a few years or months in times of revolution. According to materialist dialectics, changes in nature are due chiefly to the development of the internal contradictions in nature. Changes in society are due chiefly to the development of the internal contradictions in society, that is, the contradiction between the productive forces and the relations of production, the contradiction between classes and the contradiction between the old and the new; it is the development of these contradictions that pushes society forward and

27

gives the impetus for the supersession of the old society by the new. Does materialist dialectics exclude external causes? Not at all. It holds that external causes are the condition of change and internal causes are the basis of change, and that external causes become operative through internal causes. In a suitable temperature an egg changes into a chicken, but no temperature can change a stone into a chicken, because each has a different basis. There is constant interaction between the peoples of different countries. In the era of capitalism, and especially in the era of imperialism and proletarian revolution, the interaction and mutual impact of different countries in the political, economic and cultural spheres are extremely great. The October Socialist Revolution ushered in a new epoch in world history as well as in Russian history. It exerted influence on internal changes in the other countries in the world and, similarly and in a particularly profound way, on internal changes in China. These changes, however, were effected through the inner laws of development of these countries, China included. In battle, one army is victorious and the other is defeated; both the victory and the defeat are determined by internal causes. The one is victorious either because it is strong or because of its competent generalship, the other is vanquished either because it is weak or because of its incompetent generalship; it is through internal causes that external causes become operative. In China in 1927, the defeat of the proletariat by the big bourgeoisie came about through the opportunism then to be found within the Chinese proletariat itself (inside the Chinese Communist Party). When we liquidated this opportunism, the Chinese revolution resumed its advance. Later, the Chinese revolution again suffered severe setbacks at the hands of the enemy, because adventurism had risen within our Party. When we liquidated this adventurism, our cause advanced once again. Thus it can be seen that to lead the revolution to victory, a political party must depend on the correctness of its own political line and the solidity of its own organization.

The dialectical world outlook emerged in ancient times both in China and in Europe. Ancient dialectics, however, had a somewhat spontaneous and naive character; in the social and historical conditions then prevailing, it was not yet able to form a theoretical system, hence it could not fully explain the world and was supplanted by metaphysics. The famous German philosopher Hegel, who lived in the late 18th and early 19th centuries, made most important contributions to dialectics, but his dialectics was idealist. It was not until Marx and Engels, the great protagonists of the proletarian movement, had synthesized the positive achievements in the history of human knowledge and, in particular, critically absorbed the rational elements of Hegelian dialectics and created the great theory of dialectical and historical materialism that an unprecedented revolution occurred in the history of human knowledge. This theory was further developed by Lenin and Stalin. As soon as it spread to China, it wrought tremendous changes in the world of Chinese thought.

This dialectical world outlook teaches us primarily how to observe and analyse the movement of opposites in different things and, on the basis of such analysis, to indicate the methods for resolving contradictions. It is therefore most important for us to understand the law of contradiction in things in a concrete way.

29

II. THE UNIVERSALITY OF CONTRADICTION

For convenience of exposition, I shall deal first with the universality of contradiction and then proceed to the particularity of contradiction. The reason is that the universality of contradiction can be explained more briefly, for it has been widely recognized ever since the materialist-dialectical world outlook was discovered and materialist dialectics applied with outstanding success to analysing many aspects of human history and natural history and to changing many aspects of society and nature (as in the Soviet Union) by the great creators and continuers of Marxism — Marx, Engels, Lenin and Stalin; whereas the particularity of contradiction is still not clearly understood by many comrades, and especially by the dogmatists. They do not understand that it is precisely in the particularity of contradiction that the universality of contradiction resides. Nor do they understand how important is the study of the particularity of contradiction in the concrete things confronting us for guiding the course of revolutionary practice. Therefore, it is necessary to stress the study of the particularity of contradiction and to explain it at adequate length. For this reason, in our analysis of the law of contradiction in things, we shall first analyse the universality of contradiction, then place special stress on analysing the particularity of contradiction, and finally return to the universality of contradiction.

The universality or absoluteness of contradiction has a twofold meaning. One is that contradiction exists in the process of development of all things, and the other is that in the process of development of each thing a movement of opposites exists from beginning to end.

Engels said, "Motion itself is a contradiction."[6]   Lenin defined the law of the unity of opposites as "the recognition (discovery) of the contradictory, *mutually exclusive*, opposite tendencies in *all* phenomena and processes of nature (*including* mind and society)".[7]   Are these ideas correct? Yes, they are.   The interdependence of the contradictory aspects present in all things and the struggle between these aspects determine the life of all things and push their development forward.   There is nothing that does not contain contradiction; without contradiction nothing would exist.

Contradiction is the basis of the simple forms of motion (for instance, mechanical motion) and still more so of the complex forms of motion.

Engels explained the universality of contradiction as follows:

If simple mechanical change of place contains a contradiction, this is even more true of the higher forms of motion of matter, and especially of organic life and its development.   . . . life consists precisely and primarily in this — that a being is at each moment itself and yet something else.   Life is therefore also a contradiction which is present in things and processes themselves, and which constantly originates and resolves itself; and as soon as the contradiction ceases, life, too, comes to an end, and death steps in.   We likewise saw that also in the sphere of thought we could not escape contradictions, and that for example the contradiction between man's inherently unlimited capacity for knowledge and its actual presence only in men who are externally limited and possess limited cognition finds its solution in what is — at least practically, for us — an endless succession of generations, in infinite progress.

. . . one of the basic principles of higher mathematics is . . . contradiction. . . .

But even lower mathematics teems with contradictions.[8]

Lenin illustrated the universality of contradiction as follows:

In mathematics: $+$ and $-$. Differential and integral.
In mechanics: action and reaction.
In physics: positive and negative electricity.
In chemistry: the combination and dissociation of atoms.
In social science: the class struggle.[9]

In war, offence and defence, advance and retreat, victory and defeat are all mutually contradictory phenomena. One cannot exist without the other. The two aspects are at once in conflict and in interdependence, and this constitutes the totality of a war, pushes its development forward and solves its problems.

Every difference in men's concepts should be regarded as reflecting an objective contradiction. Objective contradictions are reflected in subjective thinking, and this process constitutes the contradictory movement of concepts, pushes forward the development of thought, and ceaselessly solves problems in man's thinking.

Opposition and struggle between ideas of different kinds constantly occur within the Party; this is a reflection within the Party of contradictions between classes and between the new and the old in society. If there were no contradictions in the Party and no ideological struggles to resolve them, the Party's life would come to an end.

Thus it is already clear that contradiction exists universally and in all processes, whether in the simple or in the complex forms of motion, whether in objective phenomena or ideological phenomena. But does contradiction also exist at the initial stage of each process? Is there a movement of opposites from beginning to end in the process of development of every single thing?

As can be seen from the articles written by Soviet philosophers criticizing it, the Deborin school maintains that contradiction appears not at the inception of a process but only when it has developed to a certain stage. If this were the case, then the cause of the development of the process before that stage would be external and not internal. Deborin thus reverts to the metaphysical theories of external causality and of mechanism. Applying this view in the analysis of concrete problems, the Deborin school sees only differences but not contradictions between the kulaks and the peasants in general under existing conditions in the Soviet Union, thus entirely agreeing with Bukharin.[10] In analysing the French Revolution, it holds that before the Revolution there were likewise only differences but not contradictions within the Third Estate, which was composed of the workers, the peasants and the bourgeoisie. These views of the Deborin school are anti-Marxist. This school does not understand that each and every difference already contains contradiction and that difference itself is contradiction. Labour and capital have been in contradiction ever since the two classes came into being, only at first the contradiction had not yet become intense. Even under the social conditions existing in the Soviet Union, there is a difference between workers and peasants and this very difference is a contradiction, although, unlike the contradiction between labour and capital, it will not become intensified into antagonism or assume the form of class struggle; the workers and the peasants have established a firm alliance in the course of socialist construction and are gradually resolving this contradiction in the course of the advance from socialism to communism. The question is one of different kinds of contradiction, not of the presence or absence of contradiction. Contradiction is universal and absolute, it is present in the process of development of all things and permeates every process from beginning to end.

What is meant by the emergence of a new process? The old unity with its constituent opposites yields to a new unity with its constituent opposites, whereupon a new process emerges to replace the old. The old process ends and the new one begins. The new process contains new contradictions and begins its own history of the development of contradictions.

As Lenin pointed out, Marx in his *Capital* gave a model analysis of this movement of opposites which runs through the process of development of things from beginning to end. This is the method that must be employed in studying the development of all things. Lenin, too, employed this method correctly and adhered to it in all his writings.

In his *Capital,* Marx first analyses the simplest, most ordinary and fundamental, most common and everyday *relation* of bourgeois (commodity) society, a relation encountered billions of times, viz. the exchange of commodities. In this very simple phenomenon (in this "cell" of bourgeois society) analysis reveals *all* the contradictions (or the germs of *all* the contradictions) of modern society. The subsequent exposition shows us the development (*both* growth *and* movement) of these contradictions and of this society in the Σ [summation] of its individual parts, from its beginning to its end.

34

Lenin added, "Such must also be the method of exposition (or study) of dialectics in general."[11]

Chinese Communists must learn this method; only then will they be able correctly to analyse the history and the present state of the Chinese revolution and infer its future.

III. THE PARTICULARITY OF CONTRADICTION

Contradiction is present in the process of development of all things; it permeates the process of development of each thing from beginning to end. This is the universality and absoluteness of contradiction which we have discussed above. Now let us discuss the particularity and relativity of contradiction.

This problem should be studied on several levels.

First, the contradiction in each form of motion of matter has its particularity. Man's knowledge of matter is knowledge of its forms of motion, because there is nothing in this world except matter in motion and this motion must assume certain forms. In considering each form of motion of matter, we must observe the points which it has in common with other forms of motion. But what is especially important and necessary, constituting as it does the foundation of our knowledge of a thing, is to observe what is particular to this form of motion of matter, namely, to observe the qualitative difference between this form of motion and other forms. Only when we have done so can we distinguish between things. Every form of motion contains within itself its own particular contradiction. This particular contradiction constitutes the particular essence which distinguishes one thing from another. It is the internal cause or, as it may be called,

35

the basis for the immense variety of things in the world. There are many forms of motion in nature, mechanical motion, sound, light, heat, electricity, dissociation, combination, and so on. All these forms are interdependent, but in its essence each is different from the others. The particular essence of each form of motion is determined by its own particular contradiction. This holds true not only for nature but also for social and ideological phenomena. Every form of society, every form of ideology, has its own particular contradiction and particular essence.

The sciences are differentiated precisely on the basis of the particular contradictions inherent in their respective objects of study. Thus the contradiction peculiar to a certain field of phenomena constitutes the object of study for a specific branch of science. For example, positive and negative numbers in mathematics; action and reaction in mechanics; positive and negative electricity in physics; dissociation and combination in chemistry; forces of production and relations of production, classes and class struggle, in social science; offence and defence in military science; idealism and materialism, the metaphysical outlook and the dialectical outlook, in philosophy; and so on — all these are the objects of study of different branches of science precisely because each branch has its own particular contradiction and particular essence. Of course, unless we understand the universality of contradiction, we have no way of discovering the universal cause or universal basis for the movement or development of things; however, unless we study the particularity of contradiction, we have no way of determining the particular essence of a thing which differentiates it from other things, no way of discovering the particular cause or particular basis for the movement or development of a thing, and

36

no way of distinguishing one thing from another or of demarcating the fields of science.

As regards the sequence in the movement of man's knowledge, there is always a gradual growth from the knowledge of individual and particular things to the knowledge of things in general. Only after man knows the particular essence of many different things can he proceed to generalization and know the common essence of things. When man attains the knowledge of this common essence, he uses it as a guide and proceeds to study various concrete things which have not yet been studied, or studied thoroughly, and to discover the particular essence of each; only thus is he able to supplement, enrich and develop his knowledge of their common essence and prevent such knowledge from withering or petrifying. These are the two processes of cognition: one, from the particular to the general, and the other, from the general to the particular. Thus cognition always moves in cycles and (so long as scientific method is strictly adhered to) each cycle advances human knowledge a step higher and so makes it more and more profound. Where our dogmatists err on this question is that, on the one hand, they do not understand that we have to study the particularity of contradiction and know the particular essence of individual things before we can adequately know the universality of contradiction and the common essence of things, and that, on the other hand, they do not understand that after knowing the common essence of things, we must go further and study the concrete things that have not yet been thoroughly studied or have only just emerged. Our dogmatists are lazy-bones. They refuse to undertake any painstaking study of concrete things, they regard general truths as emerging out of the void, they turn them into purely abstract unfathomable formulas, and thereby completely deny and reverse the normal sequence by which man comes to know truth. Nor do they understand the interconnection of the two processes in cognition — from the particular to the general and then from the general to the particular. They understand nothing of the Marxist theory of knowledge.

It is necessary not only to study the particular contradiction and the essence determined thereby of every great system of the forms of motion of matter, but also to study the particular contradiction and the essence of each process in the long course of development of each form of motion of matter. In every form of motion, each process of development which is real (and not imaginary) is qualitatively different. Our study must emphasize and start from this point.

Qualitatively different contradictions can only be resolved by qualitatively different methods. For instance, the contradiction between the proletariat and the bourgeoisie is resolved by the method of socialist revolution; the contradiction between the great masses of the people and the feudal system is resolved by the method of democratic revolution; the contradiction between the colonies and imperialism is resolved by the method of national revolutionary war; the contradiction between the working class and the peasant class in socialist society is resolved by the method of collectivization and mechanization in agriculture; contradiction within the Communist Party is resolved by the method of criticism and self-criticism; the contradiction between society and nature is resolved by the method of developing the productive forces. Processes change, old processes and old contradictions disappear, new processes and new contradictions emerge, and the methods of resolving contradictions differ accordingly. In Russia, there was a fundamental difference between the contradiction resolved by the February Revolution and the contradiction resolved by the October Revolution, as well as between the methods used to resolve them. The principle of using different methods to resolve different contradictions is one which Marxist-Leninists must strictly observe. The dogmatists do not observe this principle; they do not understand that conditions differ in different kinds of revolution and so do not understand that different methods should be used to resolve different contradictions; on the contrary, they invariably adopt what they imagine to be an unalterable formula and arbitrarily apply it everywhere, which only causes setbacks to the revolution or makes a sorry mess of what could have been done well.

In order to reveal the particularity of the contradictions in any process in the development of a thing, in their totality or interconnections, that is, in order to reveal the essence of the process, it is necessary to reveal the particularity of the two aspects of each of the contradictions in that process; otherwise it will be impossible to discover the essence of the process. This likewise requires the utmost attention in our study.

There are many contradictions in the course of development of any major thing. For instance, in the course of China's bourgeois-democratic revolution, where the conditions are exceedingly complex, there exist the contradiction between all the oppressed classes in Chinese society and imperialism, the contradiction between the great masses of the people and feudalism, the contradiction between the proletariat and the bourgeoisie, the contradiction between the peasantry and the urban petty bourgeoisie on the one hand and the bourgeoisie on the other, the contradiction between the various reactionary ruling groups, and so on. These contradictions cannot be treated in the same way since each has its own particularity; moreover, the two aspects of each contradiction cannot be treated in the same way since each aspect has its own characteristics. We who are engaged in the Chinese revolution should not only understand the particularity of these contradictions in their totality, that is, in their interconnections, but should also study the two aspects of each contradiction as the only means of understanding the totality. When we speak of understanding each aspect of a contradiction, we mean understanding what specific position each aspect occupies, what concrete forms it assumes in its interdependence and in its contradiction with its opposite, and what concrete methods are employed in the struggle with its opposite, when the two are both interdependent and in contradiction, and also after the interdependence breaks down. It is of great importance to study these problems. Lenin meant just this when he said that the most essential thing in Marxism, the living soul of Marxism, is the concrete analysis of concrete conditions.[12] Our dogmatists have violated Lenin's teachings; they never use their brains to analyse anything concretely, and in their writings and speeches they always use stereotypes devoid of content, thereby creating a very bad style of work in our Party.

In studying a problem, we must shun subjectivity, onesidedness and superficiality. To be subjective means not to look at problems objectively, that is, not to use the materialist viewpoint in looking at problems. I have discussed this in my essay "On Practice". To be one-sided means not to look at problems all-sidedly, for example, to understand only China but not Japan, only the Communist Party but not the Kuomintang, only the proletariat but not the bourgeoisie, only the peasants but not the landlords, only the favourable conditions but not the difficult ones, only the past but not the future, only individual parts but not the whole, only the defects but not the achievements, only the plaintiff's case but not the defendant's, only secret revolutionary work but not open revolutionary work, and so on. In a word, it means not to understand the characteristics of both aspects of a contradiction. This is what we mean by looking at a problem one-sidedly. Or it may be called seeing the part but not the whole, seeing the trees but not the forest. That way it is impossible to find the method for resolving a contradiction, it is impossible to accomplish the tasks of the revolution, to carry out assignments well or to develop inner-Party ideological struggle correctly. When Sun Wu Tzu said in discussing military science, "Know the enemy and know yourself, and you can fight a hundred battles with no danger of defeat",[13] he was referring to the two sides in a battle. Wei Cheng[14] of the Tang Dynasty also understood the error of one-sidedness when he said, "Listen to both sides and you will be enlightened, heed only one side and you will be benighted." But our comrades often look at problems one-sidedly, and so they often run into snags. In the novel *Shui Hu Chuan*, Sung Chiang thrice attacked Chu Village.[15] Twice he was defeated because he was ignorant of the local conditions and used the wrong method. Later he changed his method; first he investigated the situation, and he familiarized himself with the maze of roads, then he broke up the alliance between the Li, Hu and Chu Villages and sent his men in disguise into the enemy camp to lie in wait, using a stratagem similar to that of the Trojan Horse in the foreign story. And on the third occasion he won. There are many examples of materialist dialectics in *Shui Hu Chuan*, of which

41

the episode of the three attacks on Chu Village is one of the best. Lenin said:

> . . . in order really to know an object we must embrace, study, all its sides, all connections and "mediations". We shall never achieve this completely, but the demand for all-sidedness is a safeguard against mistakes and rigidity.[16]

We should remember his words. To be superficial means to consider neither the characteristics of a contradiction in its totality nor the characteristics of each of its aspects; it means to deny the necessity for probing deeply into a thing and minutely studying the characteristics of its contradiction, but instead merely to look from afar and, after glimpsing the rough outline, immediately to try to resolve the contradiction (to answer a question, settle a dispute, handle work, or direct a military operation). This way of doing things is bound to lead to trouble. The reason the dogmatist and empiricist comrades in China have made mistakes lies precisely in their subjectivist, one-sided and superficial way of looking at things. To be one-sided and superficial is at the same time to be subjective. For all objective things are actually interconnected and are governed by inner laws, but instead of undertaking the task of reflecting things as they really are some people only look at things one-sidedly or superficially and know neither their interconnections nor their inner laws, and so their method is subjectivist.

Not only does the whole process of the movement of opposites in the development of a thing, both in their interconnections and in each of the aspects, have particular features to which we must give attention, but each stage in the process has its particular features to which we must give attention too.

The fundamental contradiction in the process of development of a thing and the essence of the process determined by this fundamental contradiction will not disappear until the process is completed; but in a lengthy process the conditions usually differ at each stage. The reason is that, although the nature of the fundamental contradiction in the process of development of a thing and the essence of the process remain unchanged, the fundamental contradiction becomes more and more intensified as it passes from one stage to another in the lengthy process. In addition, among the numerous major and minor contradictions which are determined or influenced by the fundamental contradiction, some become intensified, some are temporarily or partially resolved or mitigated, and some new ones emerge; hence the process is marked by stages. If people do not pay attention to the stages in the process of development of a thing, they cannot deal with its contradictions properly.

For instance, when the capitalism of the era of free competition developed into imperialism, there was no change in the class nature of the two classes in fundamental contradiction, namely, the proletariat and the bourgeoisie, or in the capitalist essence of society; however, the contradiction between these two classes became intensified, the contradiction between monopoly and non-monopoly capital emerged, the contradiction between the colonial powers and the colonies became intensified, the contradiction among the capitalist countries resulting from their uneven development manifested itself with particular sharpness, and thus there arose the special stage of capitalism, the stage of imperialism. Leninism is the Marxism of the era of imperialism and proletarian revolution precisely because Lenin and Stalin have correctly explained these contradictions and correctly formulated the

43

theory and tactics of the proletarian revolution for their resolution.

Take the process of China's bourgeois-democratic revolution, which began with the Revolution of 1911;[17] it, too, has several distinct stages. In particular, the revolution in its period of bourgeois leadership and the revolution in its period of proletarian leadership represent two vastly different historical stages. In other words, proletarian leadership has fundamentally changed the whole face of the revolution, has brought about a new alignment of classes, given rise to a tremendous upsurge in the peasant revolution, imparted thoroughness to the revolution against imperialism and feudalism, created the possibility of the transition from the democratic revolution to the socialist revolution, and so on. None of these was possible in the period when the revolution was under bourgeois leadership. Although no change has taken place in the nature of the fundamental contradiction in the process as a whole, *i.e.*, in the anti-imperialist, anti-feudal, democratic-revolutionary nature of the process (the opposite of which is its semi-colonial and semi-feudal nature), nonetheless this process has passed through several stages of development in the course of more than twenty years; during this time many great events have taken place — the failure of the Revolution of 1911 and the establishment of the regime of the Northern warlords, the formation of the first national united front and the revolution of 1924-27,[18] the break-up of the united front and the desertion of the bourgeoisie to the side of the counter-revolution, the wars among the new warlords, the Agrarian Revolutionary War,[19] the establishment of the second national united front and the War of Resistance Against Japan. These stages are marked by particular features such as the intensification of certain contradictions (*e.g.*,

44

the Agrarian Revolutionary War and the Japanese invasion of the four northeastern provinces[20]), the partial or temporary resolution of other contradictions (*e.g.*, the destruction of the Northern warlords and our confiscation of the land of the landlords), and the emergence of yet other contradictions (*e.g.*, the conflicts among the new warlords, and the landlords' recapture of the land after the loss of our revolutionary base areas in the south).

In studying the particularities of the contradictions at each stage in the process of development of a thing, we must not only observe them in their interconnections or their totality, we must also examine the two aspects of each contradiction.

For instance, consider the Kuomintang and the Communist Party. Take one aspect, the Kuomintang. In the period of the first united front, the Kuomintang carried out Sun Yat-sen's Three Great Policies of alliance with Russia, co-operation with the Communist Party, and assistance to the peasants and workers; hence it was revolutionary and vigorous, it was an alliance of various classes for the democratic revolution. After 1927, however, the Kuomintang changed into its opposite and became a reactionary bloc of the landlords and big bourgeoisie. After the Sian Incident[21] in December 1936, it began another change in the direction of ending the civil war and co-operating with the Communist Party for joint opposition to Japanese imperialism. Such have been the particular features of the Kuomintang in the three stages. Of course, these features have arisen from a variety of causes. Now take the other aspect, the Chinese Communist Party. In the period of the first united front, the Chinese Communist Party was in its infancy; it courageously led the revolution of 1924-27 but revealed its immaturity in its understanding of the character, the tasks and the methods of the revolution, and consequently it became possible for Chen Tu-hsiuism,[22] which appeared during the latter part of this revolution, to assert itself and bring about the defeat of the revolution. After 1927, the Communist Party courageously led the Agrarian Revolutionary War and created the revolutionary army and revolutionary base areas; however, it committed adventurist errors which brought about very great losses both to the army and to the base areas. Since 1935 the Party has corrected these errors and has been leading the new united front for resistance to Japan; this great struggle is now developing. At the present stage, the Communist Party is a Party that has gone through the test of two revolutions and acquired a wealth of experience. Such have been the particular features of the Chinese Communist Party in the three stages. These features, too, have arisen from a variety of causes. Without studying both these sets of features we cannot understand the particular relations between the two parties during the various stages of their development, namely, the establishment of a united front, the break-up of the united front, and the establishment of another united front. What is even more fundamental for the study of the particular features of the two parties is the examination of the class basis of the two parties and the resultant contradictions which have arisen between each party and other forces at different periods. For instance, in the period of its first co-operation with the Communist Party, the Kuomintang stood in contradiction to foreign imperialism and was therefore anti-imperialist; on the other hand, it stood in contradiction to the great masses of the people within the country — although in words it promised many benefits to the working people, in fact it gave them little or nothing. In the period when it carried on the anti-Communist war, the Kuomintang collaborated with imperialism and feudalism against the great masses of the people and wiped out all the gains they had won in the revolution, and thereby intensified its contradictions with them. In the present period of the anti-Japanese war, the Kuomintang stands in contradiction to Japanese imperialism and wants co-operation with the Communist Party, without however relaxing its struggle against the Communist Party and the people or its oppression of them. As for the Communist Party, it has always, in every period, stood with the great masses of the people against imperialism and feudalism, but in the present period of the anti-Japanese war, it has adopted a moderate policy towards the Kuomintang and the domestic feudal forces because the Kuomintang has expressed itself in favour of resisting Japan. The above circumstances have resulted now in alliance between the two parties and now in struggle between them, and even during the periods of alliance there has been a complicated state of simultaneous alliance and struggle. If we do not study the particular features of both aspects of the contradiction, we shall fail to understand not only the relations of each party with the other forces, but also the relations between the two parties.

It can thus be seen that in studying the particularity of any kind of contradiction — the contradiction in each form of motion of matter, the contradiction in each of its processes of development, the two aspects of the contradiction in each process, the contradiction at each stage of a process, and the two aspects of the contradiction at each stage — in studying the particularity of all these contradictions, we must not be subjective and arbitrary but must analyse it concretely. Without concrete analysis there can be no knowledge of the particularity of any contradiction. We must always remember Lenin's words, the concrete analysis of concrete conditions.

Marx and Engels were the first to provide us with excellent models of such concrete analysis.

When Marx and Engels applied the law of contradiction in things to the study of the socio-historical process, they discovered the contradiction between the productive forces and the relations of production, they discovered the contradiction between the exploiting and exploited classes and also the resultant contradiction between the economic base and its superstructure (politics, ideology, etc.), and they discovered how these contradictions inevitably lead to different kinds of social revolution in different kinds of class society.

When Marx applied this law to the study of the economic structure of capitalist society, he discovered that the basic contradiction of this society is the contradiction between the social character of production and the private character of ownership. This contradiction manifests itself in the contradiction between the organized character of production in individual enterprises and the anarchic character of production in society as a whole. In terms of class relations, it manifests itself in the contradiction between the bourgeoisie and the proletariat.

Because the range of things is vast and there is no limit to their development, what is universal in one context becomes particular in another. Conversely, what is particular in one context becomes universal in another. The contradiction in the capitalist system between the social character of production and the private ownership of the means of production is common to all countries where capitalism exists and develops; as far as capitalism is concerned, this constitutes the universality of contradiction. But this contradiction of capitalism belongs only to a certain historical stage in the general development of class society; as far as the contradiction between the productive forces and the relations of production in class society as a whole is concerned, it constitutes the particularity of contradiction. However, in the course of dissecting the particularity of all these contradictions in capitalist society, Marx gave a still more profound, more adequate and more complete elucidation of the universality of the contradiction between the productive forces and the relations of production in class society in general.

Since the particular is united with the universal and since the universality as well as the particularity of contradiction is inherent in everything, universality residing in particularity, we should, when studying an object, try to discover both the particular and the universal and their interconnection, to discover both particularity and universality and also their interconnection within the object itself, and to discover the interconnections of this object with the many objects outside it. When Stalin explained the historical roots of Leninism in his famous work, *The Foundations of Leninism,* he analysed the international situation in which Leninism arose, analysed those contradictions of capitalism which reached their culmination under imperialism, and showed how these contradictions made proletarian revolution a matter for immediate action and created favourable conditions for a direct onslaught on capitalism. What is more, he analysed the reasons why Russia became the cradle of Leninism, why tsarist Russia became the focus of all the contradictions of imperialism, and why it was possible for the Russian proletariat to become the vanguard of the international revolutionary proletariat. Thus, Stalin analysed the universality of contradiction in imperialism, showing why Leninism is the

Marxism of the era of imperialism and proletarian revolution, and at the same time analysed the particularity of tsarist Russian imperialism within this general contradiction, showing why Russia became the birthplace of the theory and tactics of proletarian revolution and how the universality of contradiction is contained in this particularity. Stalin's analysis provides us with a model for understanding the particularity and the universality of contradiction and their interconnection.

On the question of using dialectics in the study of objective phenomena, Marx and Engels, and likewise Lenin and Stalin, always enjoin people not to be in any way subjective and arbitrary but, from the concrete conditions in the actual objective movement of these phenomena, to discover their concrete contradictions, the concrete position of each aspect of every contradiction and the concrete interrelations of the contradictions. Our dogmatists do not have this attitude in study and therefore can never get anything right. We must take warning from their failure and learn to acquire this attitude, which is the only correct one in study.

The relationship between the universality and the particularity of contradiction is the relationship between the general character and the individual character of contradiction. By the former we mean that contradiction exists in and runs through all processes from beginning to end; motion, things, processes, thinking — all are contradictions. To deny contradiction is to deny everything. This is a universal truth for all times and all countries, which admits of no exception. Hence the general character, the absoluteness of contradiction. But this general character is contained in every individual character; without individual character there can be no general character. If all individual character were removed, what general character would remain? It is because each contradiction is particular that individual character arises. All individual character exists conditionally and temporarily, and hence is relative.

This truth concerning general and individual character, concerning absoluteness and relativity, is the quintessence of the problem of contradiction in things; failure to understand it is tantamount to abandoning dialectics.

IV. THE PRINCIPAL CONTRADICTION AND THE PRINCIPAL ASPECT OF A CONTRADICTION

There are still two points in the problem of the particularity of contradiction which must be singled out for analysis, namely, the principal contradiction and the principal aspect of a contradiction.

There are many contradictions in the process of development of a complex thing, and one of them is necessarily the principal contradiction whose existence and development determine or influence the existence and development of the other contradictions.

For instance, in capitalist society the two forces in contradiction, the proletariat and the bourgeoisie, form the principal contradiction. The other contradictions, such as those between the remnant feudal class and the bourgeoisie, between the peasant petty bourgeoisie and the bourgeoisie, between the proletariat and the peasant petty bourgeoisie, between the non-monopoly capitalists and the monopoly capitalists, between bourgeois democracy and bourgeois fascism, among the capitalist countries and between imperialism and the colonies, are all determined or influenced by this principal contradiction.

In a semi-colonial country such as China, the relationship between the principal contradiction and the non-principal contradictions presents a complicated picture.

When imperialism launches a war of aggression against such a country, all its various classes, except for some traitors, can temporarily unite in a national war against imperialism. At such a time, the contradiction between imperialism and the country concerned becomes the principal contradiction, while all the contradictions among the various classes within the country (including what was the principal contradiction, between the feudal system and the great masses of the people) are temporarily relegated to a secondary and subordinate position. So it was in China in the Opium War of 1840,[23] the Sino-Japanese War of 1894[24] and the Yi Ho Tuan War of 1900, and so it is now in the present Sino-Japanese War.

But in another situation, the contradictions change position. When imperialism carries on its oppression not by war, but by milder means — political, economic and cultural — the ruling classes in semi-colonial countries capitulate to imperialism, and the two form an alliance for the joint oppression of the masses of the people. At such a time, the masses often resort to civil war against the alliance of imperialism and the feudal classes, while imperialism often employs indirect methods rather than direct action in helping the reactionaries in the semi-colonial countries to oppress the people, and thus the internal contradictions become particularly sharp. This is what happened in China in the Revolutionary War of 1911, the Revolutionary War of 1924-27, and the ten years of Agrarian Revolutionary War after 1927. Wars among the various reactionary ruling groups in the semi-colonial countries, e.g., the wars among the warlords in China, fall into the same category.

When a revolutionary civil war develops to the point of threatening the very existence of imperialism and its running dogs, the domestic reactionaries, imperialism often adopts other methods in order to maintain its rule; it either tries to split the revolutionary front from within or sends armed forces to help the domestic reactionaries directly. At such a time, foreign imperialism and domestic reaction stand quite openly at one pole while the masses of the people stand at the other pole, thus forming the principal contradiction which determines or influences the development of the other contradictions. The assistance given by various capitalist countries to the Russian reactionaries after the October Revolution is an example of armed intervention. Chiang Kai-shek's betrayal in 1927 is an example of splitting the revolutionary front.

But whatever happens, there is no doubt at all that at every stage in the development of a process, there is only one principal contradiction which plays the leading role.

Hence, if in any process there are a number of contradictions, one of them must be the principal contradiction playing the leading and decisive role, while the rest occupy a secondary and subordinate position. Therefore, in studying any complex process in which there are two or more contradictions, we must devote every effort to finding its principal contradiction. Once this principal contradiction is grasped, all problems can be readily solved. This is the method Marx taught us in his study of capitalist society. Likewise Lenin and Stalin taught us this method when they studied imperialism and the general crisis of capitalism and when they studied the Soviet economy. There are thousands of scholars and men of action who do not understand it, and the result is that, lost in a fog, they are unable to get to the heart of a problem and naturally cannot find a way to resolve its contradictions.

As we have said, one must not treat all the contradictions in a process as being equal but must distinguish between the principal and the secondary contradictions, and pay special attention to grasping the principal one. But, in any given contradiction, whether principal or secondary, should the two contradictory aspects be treated as equal? Again, no. In any contradiction the development of the contradictory aspects is uneven. Sometimes they seem to be in equilibrium, which is however only temporary and relative, while unevenness is basic. Of the two contradictory aspects, one must be principal and the other secondary. The principal aspect is the one playing the leading role in the contradiction. The nature of a thing is determined mainly by the principal aspect of a contradiction, the aspect which has gained the dominant position.

But this situation is not static; the principal and the non-principal aspects of a contradiction transform themselves into each other and the nature of the thing changes accordingly. In a given process or at a given stage in the development of a contradiction, A is the principal aspect and B is the non-principal aspect; at another stage or in another process the roles are reversed — a change determined by the extent of the increase or decrease in the force of each aspect in its struggle against the other in the course of the development of a thing.

We often speak of "the new superseding the old". The supersession of the old by the new is a general, eternal and inviolable law of the universe. The transformation of one thing into another, through leaps of different forms in accordance with its essence and external conditions — this is the process of the new superseding the old. In each thing there is contradiction between its new and its old aspects, and this gives rise to a series of struggles with many twists and turns. As a result of these struggles, the new aspect changes from being minor to being major and rises to predominance, while the old aspect changes from being major to being minor and gradually dies out. And the moment the new aspect gains dominance over the old, the old thing changes qualitatively into a new thing. It can thus be seen that the nature of a thing is mainly determined by the principal aspect of the contradiction, the aspect which has gained predominance. When the principal aspect which has gained predominance changes, the nature of a thing changes accordingly.

In capitalist society, capitalism has changed its position from being a subordinate force in the old feudal era to being the dominant force, and the nature of society has accordingly changed from feudal to capitalist. In the new, capitalist era, the feudal forces changed from their former dominant position to a subordinate one, gradually dying out. Such was the case, for example, in Britain and France. With the development of the productive forces, the bourgeoisie changes from being a new class playing a progressive role to being an old class playing a reactionary role, until it is finally overthrown by the proletariat and becomes a class deprived of privately owned means of production and stripped of power, when it, too, gradually dies out. The proletariat, which is much more numerous than the bourgeoisie and grows simultaneously with it but under its rule, is a new force which, initially subordinate to the bourgeoisie, gradually gains strength, becomes an independent class playing the leading role in history, and finally seizes political power and becomes the ruling class. Thereupon the nature of society changes and the old capitalist society becomes the new socialist society. This is the path already taken by the Soviet Union, a path that all other countries will inevitably take.

Look at China, for instance. Imperialism occupies the principal position in the contradiction in which China has been reduced to a semi-colony, it oppresses the Chinese people, and China has been changed from an independent country into a semi-colonial one. But this state of affairs will inevitably change; in the struggle between the two sides, the power of the Chinese people which is growing under the leadership of the proletariat will inevitably change China from a semi-colony into an independent country, whereas imperialism will be overthrown and old China will inevitably change into New China.

The change of old China into New China also involves a change in the relation between the old feudal forces and the new popular forces within the country. The old feudal landlord class will be overthrown, and from being the ruler it will change into being the ruled; and this class, too, will gradually die out. From being the ruled the people, led by the proletariat, will become the rulers. Thereupon, the nature of Chinese society will change and the old, semi-colonial and semi-feudal society will change into a new democratic society.

Instances of such reciprocal transformation are found in our past experience. The Ching Dynasty which ruled China for nearly three hundred years was overthrown in the Revolution of 1911, and the revolutionary *Tung Meng Hui* under Sun Yat-sen's leadership was victorious for a time. In the Revolutionary War of 1924-27, the revolutionary forces of the Communist-Kuomintang alliance in the south changed from being weak to being strong and won victory in the Northern

Expedition, while the Northern warlords who once ruled the roost were overthrown. In 1927, the people's forces led by the Communist Party were greatly reduced numerically under the attacks of Kuomintang reaction, but with the elimination of opportunism within their ranks they gradually grew again. In the revolutionary base areas under Communist leadership, the peasants have been transformed from being the ruled to being the rulers, while the landlords have undergone a reverse transformation. It is always so in the world, the new displacing the old, the old being superseded by the new, the old being eliminated to make way for the new, and the new emerging out of the old.

At certain times in the revolutionary struggle, the difficulties outweigh the favourable conditions and so constitute the principal aspect of the contradiction and the favourable conditions constitute the secondary aspect. But through their efforts the revolutionaries can overcome the difficulties step by step and open up a favourable new situation; thus a difficult situation yields place to a favourable one. This is what happened after the failure of the revolution in China in 1927 and during the Long March of the Chinese Red Army. In the present Sino-Japanese War, China is again in a difficult position, but we can change this and fundamentally transform the situation as between China and Japan. Conversely, favourable conditions can be transformed into difficulty if the revolutionaries make mistakes. Thus the victory of the revolution of 1924-27 turned into defeat. The revolutionary base areas which grew up in the southern provinces after 1927 had all suffered defeat by 1934.

When we engage in study, the same holds good for the contradiction in the passage from ignorance to knowledge. At the very beginning of our study of Marxism, our ignorance of or scanty acquaintance with Marxism stands in contradiction to knowledge of Marxism. But by assiduous study, ignorance can be transformed into knowledge, scanty knowledge into substantial knowledge, and blindness in the application of Marxism into mastery of its application.

Some people think that this is not true of certain contradictions. For instance, in the contradiction between the productive forces and the relations of production, the productive forces are the principal aspect; in the contradiction between theory and practice, practice is the principal aspect; in the contradiction between the economic base and the superstructure, the economic base is the principal aspect; and there is no change in their respective positions. This is the mechanical materialist conception, not the dialectical materialist conception. True, the productive forces, practice and the economic base generally play the principal and decisive role; whoever denies this is not a materialist. But it must also be admitted that in certain conditions, such aspects as the relations of production, theory and the superstructure in turn manifest themselves in the principal and decisive role. When it is impossible for the productive forces to develop without a change in the relations of production, then the change in the relations of production plays the principal and decisive role. The creation and advocacy of revolutionary theory plays the principal and decisive role in those times of which Lenin said, "Without revolutionary theory there can be no revolutionary movement." When a task, no matter which, has to be performed, but there is as yet no guiding line, method, plan or policy, the principal and decisive thing is to decide on a guiding line, method, plan or policy. When the superstructure (politics, culture, etc.) obstructs the development of the economic base, political and cultural changes become principal and decisive. Are we going against materialism when we say this? No. The reason is that while we recognize that in the general development of history the material determines the mental and social being determines social consciousness, we also — and indeed must — recognize the reaction of mental on material things, of social consciousness on social being and of the superstructure on the economic base. This does not go against materialism; on the contrary, it avoids mechanical materialism and firmly upholds dialectical materialism.

In studying the particularity of contradiction, unless we examine these two facets — the principal and the non-principal contradictions in a process, and the principal and the non-principal aspects of a contradiction — that is, unless we examine the distinctive character of these two facets of contradiction, we shall get bogged down in abstractions, be unable to understand contradiction concretely and consequently be unable to find the correct method of resolving it. The distinctive character or particularity of these two facets of contradiction represents the unevenness of the forces that are in contradiction. Nothing in this world develops absolutely evenly; we must oppose the theory of even development or the theory of equilibrium. Moreover, it is these concrete features of a contradiction and the changes in the principal and non-principal aspects of a contradiction in the course of its development that manifest the force of the new superseding the old. The study of the various states of unevenness in contradictions, of the principal and non-principal contradictions and of the principal and the non-principal aspects of a contradiction constitutes an essential method by which a revolutionary political party correctly determines its strategic and tactical policies both in political and in military affairs. All Communists must give it attention.

V. THE IDENTITY AND STRUGGLE OF THE ASPECTS OF A CONTRADICTION

When we understand the universality and the particularity of contradiction, we must proceed to study the problem of the identity and struggle of the aspects of a contradiction.

Identity, unity, coincidence, interpenetration, interpermeation, interdependence (or mutual dependence for existence), interconnection or mutual co-operation — all these different terms mean the same thing and refer to the following two points: first, the existence of each of the two aspects of a contradiction in the process of the development of a thing presupposes the existence of the other aspect, and both aspects coexist in a single entity; second, in given conditions, each of the two contradictory aspects transforms itself into its opposite. This is the meaning of identity.

Lenin said:

Dialectics is the teaching which shows how *opposites* can be and how they happen to be (how they become) *identical* — under what conditions they are identical, transforming themselves into one another, — why the human mind should take these opposites not as dead, rigid, but as living, conditional, mobile, transforming themselves into one another.[25]

What does this passage mean?

The contradictory aspects in every process exclude each other, struggle with each other and are in opposition to each other. Without exception, they are contained in the process of development of all things and in all human thought. A simple process contains only a single pair of opposites, while a complex process contains more. And in turn, the pairs of opposites are in contradiction to one another. That is how all things in the objective world and all human thought are constituted and how they are set in motion.

This being so, there is an utter lack of identity or unity. How then can one speak of identity or unity?

The fact is that no contradictory aspect can exist in isolation. Without its opposite aspect, each loses the condition for its existence. Just think, can any one contradictory aspect of a thing or of a concept in the human mind exist independently? Without life, there would be no death; without death, there would be no life. Without "above", there would be no "below"; without "below", there would be no "above". Without misfortune, there would be no good fortune; without good fortune, there would be no misfortune. Without facility, there would be no difficulty; without difficulty, there would be no facility. Without landlords, there would be no tenant-peasants; without tenant-peasants, there would be no landlords. Without the bourgeoisie, there would be no proletariat; without the proletariat, there would be no bourgeoisie. Without imperialist oppression of nations, there would be no colonies or semi-colonies; without colonies or semi-colonies, there would be no imperialist oppression of nations. It is so with all opposites; in given conditions, on the one hand they are opposed to each other, and on the other they are interconnected, interpenetrating, interpermeating and interdependent, and this character is described as identity. In given conditions, all contradictory aspects possess the character of non-identity and hence are described as being in contradiction. But they also possess the character of identity and hence are interconnected. This is what Lenin means when he says that dialectics studies "how *opposites* can be . . . *identical*". How then can they be identical? Because each is the condition for the other's existence. This is the first meaning of identity.

But is it enough to say merely that each of the contradictory aspects is the condition for the other's existence, that there is identity between them and that consequently they can coexist in a single entity? No, it is not. The matter does not end with their dependence on each other for their existence; what is more important is their transformation into each other. That is to say, in given conditions, each of the contradictory aspects within a thing transforms itself into its opposite, changes its position to that of its opposite. This is the second meaning of the identity of contradiction.

Why is there identity here, too? You see, by means of revolution the proletariat, at one time the ruled, is transformed into the ruler, while the bourgeoisie, the erstwhile ruler, is transformed into the ruled and changes its position to that originally occupied by its opposite. This has already taken place in the Soviet Union, as it will take place throughout the world. If there were no interconnection and identity of opposites in given conditions, how could such a change take place?

The Kuomintang, which played a certain positive role at a certain stage in modern Chinese history, became a counter-revolutionary party after 1927 because of its inherent class nature and because of imperialist blandishments (these being the conditions); but it has been compelled to agree to resist Japan because of the sharpening of the contradiction between China and Japan and because of the Communist Party's policy of the united front (these being the conditions). Things in contradiction change into one another, and herein lies a definite identity.

Our agrarian revolution has been a process in which the landlord class owning the land is transformed into a class that has lost its land, while the peasants who once lost their land are transformed into small holders who have acquired land, and it will be such a process once again. In given conditions having and not having, acquiring and losing, are interconnected; there is identity of the two sides. Under socialism, private peasant ownership is transformed into the public ownership of socialist agriculture; this has already taken place in the Soviet Union, as it will take place everywhere else. There is a bridge leading from private property to public property, which in philosophy is called identity, or transformation into each other, or interpenetration.

To consolidate the dictatorship of the proletariat or the dictatorship of the people is in fact to prepare the conditions for abolishing this dictatorship and advancing to the higher stage when all state systems are eliminated. To establish and build the Communist Party is in fact to prepare the conditions for the elimination of the Communist Party and all political parties. To build a revolutionary army under the leadership of the Communist Party and to carry on revolutionary war is in fact to prepare the conditions for the permanent elimination of war. These opposites are at the same time complementary.

War and peace, as everybody knows, transform themselves into each other. War is transformed into peace; for instance, the First World War was transformed into the post-war peace, and the civil war in China has now stopped, giving place to internal peace. Peace is transformed into war; for instance, the Kuomintang-Communist co-operation was transformed into war in 1927, and today's situation of world peace may be transformed into a second world war. Why is this so? Because in class society such contradictory things as war and peace have an identity in given conditions.

All contradictory things are interconnected; not only do they coexist in a single entity in given conditions, but in other given conditions, they also transform themselves into each other. This is the full meaning of the identity of opposites. This is what Lenin meant when he discussed "how they happen to be (how they become) *identical* — under what conditions they are identical, transforming themselves into one another".

Why is it that "the human mind should take these opposites not as dead, rigid, but as living, conditional, mobile, transforming themselves into one another"? Because that is just how things are in objective reality. The fact is that the unity or identity of opposites in objective things is not dead or rigid, but is living, conditional, mobile, temporary and relative; in given conditions, every contradictory aspect transforms itself into its opposite. Reflected in man's thinking, this becomes the Marxist world outlook of materialist dialectics. It is only the reactionary ruling classes of the past and present and the metaphysicians in their service who regard opposites not as living, conditional, mobile and transforming themselves into one another, but as dead and rigid, and they propagate this fallacy everywhere to delude the masses of the people, thus seeking to perpetuate their rule. The task of Communists is to expose the fallacies of the reactionaries and metaphysicians, to propagate the dialectics inherent in things, and so accelerate the transformation of things and achieve the goal of revolution.

In speaking of the identity of opposites in given conditions, what we are referring to is real and concrete opposites and the real and concrete transformations of opposites into one another. There are innumerable transformations in mythology, for instance, Kua Fu's race with the sun in *Shan Hai Ching*,[26] Yi's shooting down of nine suns in *Huai Nan Tzu*,[27] the Monkey King's seventy-two metamorphoses in *Hsi Yu Chi*,[28] the numerous episodes of ghosts and foxes metamorphosed into human beings in the *Strange Tales of Liao Chai*,[29] etc. But these legendary transformations of opposites are not concrete changes reflecting concrete contradictions. They are naive, imaginary, subjectively conceived transformations conjured up in men's minds by innumerable real and complex transformations of opposites into one another. Marx said, "All mythology masters and dominates and shapes the forces of nature in and through the imagination; hence it disappears as soon as man gains mastery over the forces of nature."[30] The myriads of changes in mythology (and also in nursery tales) delight people because they imaginatively picture man's conquest of the forces of nature, and the best myths possess "eternal charm", as Marx put it; but myths are not built out of the concrete contradictions existing in given conditions and therefore are not a scientific reflection of reality. That is to say, in myths or nursery tales the aspects constituting a contradiction have only an imaginary identity, not a concrete identity. The scientific reflection of the identity in real transformations is Marxist dialectics.

Why can an egg but not a stone be transformed into a chicken? Why is there identity between war and peace and none between war and a stone? Why can human beings give birth only to human beings and not to anything else? The sole reason is that the identity of opposites exists only in necessary given conditions. Without these necessary given conditions there can be no identity whatsoever.

Why is it that in Russia in 1917 the bourgeois-democratic February Revolution was directly linked with the proletarian socialist October Revolution, while in France the bourgeois revolution was not directly linked with a socialist revolution and the Paris Commune of 1871[31] ended in failure? Why is it, on the other hand, that the nomadic system of Mongolia and Central Asia has been directly linked with socialism? Why is it that the Chinese revolution can avoid a capitalist future and be directly linked with socialism without taking the old historical road of the Western countries, without passing through a period of bourgeois dictatorship? The sole reason is the concrete conditions of the time. When certain necessary conditions are present, certain contradictions arise in the process of development of things and, moreover, the opposites contained in them are interdependent and become transformed into one another; otherwise none of this would be possible.

Such is the problem of identity. What then is struggle? And what is the relation between identity and struggle?

Lenin said:

> The unity (coincidence, identity, equal action) of opposites is conditional, temporary, transitory, relative. The struggle of mutually exclusive opposites is absolute, just as development and motion are absolute.[32]

What does this passage mean?

All processes have a beginning and an end, all processes transform themselves into their opposites. The constancy of all processes is relative, but the mutability manifested in the transformation of one process into another is absolute.

There are two states of motion in all things, that of relative rest and that of conspicuous change. Both are caused by the struggle between the two contradictory elements contained in a thing. When the thing is in the first state of motion, it is undergoing only quantitative and not qualitative change and consequently presents the outward appearance of being at rest. When the thing is in the second state of motion, the quantitative change of the first state has already reached a culminating point and gives rise to the dissolution of the thing as an entity and thereupon a qualitative change ensues, hence the appearance of a conspicuous change. Such unity, solidarity, combination, harmony, balance, stalemate, deadlock, rest, constancy, equilibrium, solidity, attraction, etc., as we see in daily life, are all the appearances of things in the state of quantitative change. On the other hand, the dissolution of unity, that is, the destruction of this solidarity, combination, harmony, balance, stalemate, deadlock, rest, constancy, equilibrium, solidity and attraction, and the change of each into its opposite are all the appearances of things in the state of qualitative change, the transformation of one process into another. Things are constantly transforming themselves from the first into the second state of motion; the struggle of opposites goes on in both states but the contradiction is resolved through the second state. That is why we say that the unity of opposites is conditional, temporary and relative, while the struggle of mutually exclusive opposites is absolute.

When we said above that two opposite things can coexist in a single entity and can transform themselves into each other because there is identity between them, we were speaking of conditionality, that is to say, in given conditions two contradictory things can be united and can transform themselves into each other, but in the absence of these conditions, they cannot constitute a contradiction, cannot coexist in the same entity and cannot transform themselves into one another. It is because the identity of opposites obtains only in given conditions that we have said identity is conditional and relative. We may add that the struggle between opposites permeates a process from beginning to end and makes one process transform itself into another, that it is ubiquitous, and that struggle is therefore unconditional and absolute.

The combination of conditional, relative identity and unconditional, absolute struggle constitutes the movement of opposites in all things.

We Chinese often say, "Things that oppose each other also complement each other."[33] That is, things opposed to each other have identity. This saying is dialectical and contrary to metaphysics. "Oppose each other" refers to the mutual exclusion or the struggle of two contradictory aspects. "Complement each other" means that in given conditions the two contradictory aspects unite and achieve identity. Yet struggle is inherent in identity and without struggle there can be no identity.

In identity there is struggle, in particularity there is universality, and in individuality there is generality. To quote Lenin, "... there *is* an absolute *in* the relative."[34]

VI. THE PLACE OF ANTAGONISM IN CONTRADICTION

The question of the struggle of opposites includes the question of what is antagonism. Our answer is that antagonism is one form, but not the only form, of the struggle of opposites.

In human history, antagonism between classes exists as a particular manifestation of the struggle of opposites. Consider the contradiction between the exploiting and the exploited classes. Such contradictory classes coexist for a long time in the same society, be it slave society, feudal society or capitalist society, and they struggle with each other; but it is not until the contradiction between the two classes develops to a certain stage that it assumes the form of open antagonism and develops into revolution. The same holds for the transformation of peace into war in class society.

Before it explodes, a bomb is a single entity in which opposites coexist in given conditions. The explosion takes place only when a new condition, ignition, is present. An analogous situation arises in all those natural phenomena which finally assume the form of open conflict to resolve old contradictions and produce new things.

It is highly important to grasp this fact. It enables us to understand that revolutions and revolutionary wars are inevitable in class society and that without them, it is impossible to accomplish any leap in social development and to overthrow the reactionary ruling classes and therefore impossible for the people to win political power. Communists must expose the deceitful propaganda of the reactionaries, such as the assertion that social revolution is unnecessary and impossible. They must firmly uphold the Marxist-Leninist theory of social revolution and enable the people to understand that social revolution is not only entirely necessary but also entirely practicable, and that the whole history of mankind and the triumph of the Soviet Union have confirmed this scientific truth.

However, we must make a concrete study of the circumstances of each specific struggle of opposites and should not arbitrarily apply the formula discussed above to everything. Contradiction and struggle are universal and absolute, but the methods of resolving contradictions, that is, the forms of struggle, differ according to the differences in the nature of the contradictions. Some contradictions are characterized by open antagonism, others are not. In accordance with the concrete development of things, some contradictions which were originally non-antagonistic develop into antagonistic ones, while others which were originally antagonistic develop into non-antagonistic ones.

As already mentioned, so long as classes exist, contradictions between correct and incorrect ideas in the Communist Party are reflections within the Party of class contradictions. At first, with regard to certain issues, such contradictions may not manifest themselves as antagonistic. But with the development of the class struggle, they may grow and become antagonistic. The history of the Communist Party of the Soviet Union shows us that the contradictions between the correct thinking of Lenin and Stalin and the fallacious thinking of Trotsky,[35] Bukharin and others did not at first manifest themselves in an antagonistic form, but that later they did develop into antagonism. There are similar cases in the history of the Chinese Communist Party. At first the contradictions between the correct thinking of many of our Party comrades and the fallacious thinking of Chen Tu-hsiu, Chang Kuo-tao and others also did not manifest themselves in an antagonistic form, but later they did develop into antagonism. At present the contradiction between correct and incorrect thinking in our Party does not manifest itself in an antagonistic form, and if comrades who have committed mistakes can correct them, it will not develop into antagonism.

Therefore, the Party must on the one hand wage a serious struggle against erroneous thinking, and on the other give the comrades who have committed errors ample opportunity to wake up. This being the case, excessive struggle is obviously inappropriate. But if the people who have committed errors persist in them and aggravate them, there is the possibility that this contradiction will develop into antagonism.

Economically, the contradiction between town and country is an extremely antagonistic one both in capitalist society, where under the rule of the bourgeoisie the towns ruthlessly plunder the countryside, and in the Kuomintang areas in China, where under the rule of foreign imperialism and the Chinese big comprador bourgeoisie the towns most rapaciously plunder the countryside. But in a socialist country and in our revolutionary base areas, this antagonistic contradiction has changed into one that is non-antagonistic; and when communist society is reached it will be abolished.

Lenin said, "Antagonism and contradiction are not at all one and the same. Under socialism, the first will disappear, the second will remain."[36] That is to say, antagonism is one form, but not the only form, of the struggle of opposites; the formula of antagonism cannot be arbitrarily applied everywhere.

VII. CONCLUSION

We may now say a few words to sum up. The law of contradiction in things, that is, the law of the unity of opposites, is the fundamental law of nature and of society and therefore also the fundamental law of thought. It stands opposed to the metaphysical world outlook. It represents a great revolution in the history of human knowledge. According to dialectical materialism, contradiction is present in all processes of objectively existing things and of subjective thought and permeates all these processes from beginning to end; this is the universality and absoluteness of contradiction. Each contradiction and each of its aspects have their respective characteristics; this is the particularity and relativity of contradiction. In given conditions, opposites possess identity, and consequently can coexist in a single entity and can transform themselves into each other; this again is the particularity and relativity of contradiction. But the struggle of opposites is ceaseless, it goes on both when the opposites are coexisting and when they are transforming themselves into each other, and becomes especially conspicuous when they are transforming themselves into one another; this again is the universality and absoluteness of contradiction. In studying the particularity and relativity of contradiction, we must give attention to the distinction between the principal contradiction and the non-principal contradictions and to the distinction between the principal aspect and the non-principal aspect of a contradiction; in studying the universality of contradiction and the struggle of opposites in contradiction, we must give attention to the distinction between the different forms of struggle. Otherwise we shall make mistakes. If, through study, we achieve a real understanding of the essentials explained above, we shall be able to demolish dogmatist ideas which are contrary to the basic principles of Marxism-Leninism and detrimental to our revolutionary cause, and our comrades with practical experience will be able to organize their experience into principles and avoid repeating empiricist errors. These are a few simple conclusions from our study of the law of contradiction.

NOTES

[1] From Lenin's notes on "The Eleatic School" in Hegel's *Lectures on the History of Philosophy*, Vol. I. See V. I. Lenin, "Conspectus of Hegel's *Lectures on the History of Philosophy*" (1915), *Collected Works*, Russ. ed., Moscow, 1958, Vol. XXXVIII, p. 249.

[2] In his essay "On the Question of Dialectics" (1915), Lenin said, "The splitting in two of a single whole and the cognition of its contradictory parts (see the quotation from Philo on Heraclitus at the beginning of Section 3 'On Cognition' in Lassalle's book on Heraclitus) is the *essence* (one of the 'essentials', one of the principal, if not the principal, characteristics or features) of dialectics." (*Collected Works*, Russ. ed., Moscow, 1958, Vol. XXXVIII, p. 357.) In his "Conspectus of Hegel's *The Science of Logic*" (September-December 1914), he said, "In brief, dialectics can be defined as the doctrine of the unity of opposites. This grasps the kernel of dialectics, but it requires explanations and development." (*Ibid.*, p. 215.)

[3] Deborin (1881-1963), a Soviet philosopher, was a member of the Academy of Sciences of the USSR. In 1930 philosophical circles in the Soviet Union began to criticize the Deborin school and pointed out that its errors in separating theory from practice and philosophy from politics were idealist in nature.

[4] V. I. Lenin, "On the Question of Dialectics", *Collected Works*, Russ. ed., Moscow, 1958, Vol. XXXVIII, p. 358.

[5] A saying of Tung Chung-shu (179-104 B.C.), a well-known exponent of Confucianism in the Han Dynasty.

[6] Frederick Engels, "Dialectics. Quantity and Quality", *Anti-Dühring* (1877-78), Eng. ed., FLPH, Moscow, 1959, p. 166.

[7] V. I. Lenin, "On the Question of Dialectics", *Collected Works*, Russ. ed., Moscow, 1958, Vol. XXXVIII, pp. 357-58.

[8] Frederick Engels, *op. cit.*, pp. 166-67.

[9] V. I. Lenin, "On the Question of Dialectics", *Collected Works*, Russ. ed., Moscow, 1958, Vol. XXXVIII, p. 357.

[10] Bukharin (1888-1938) headed an anti-Leninist faction in the Russian revolutionary movement. Later he joined a traitorous group, was expelled from the Party in 1937, and sentenced to death by the Soviet Supreme Court in 1938. Here Comrade Mao Tse-tung criticized the erroneous view, which had long been advocated by Bukharin, of covering up class contradictions and substituting class collaboration for class struggle. In the years 1928-29 when the Soviet Union was preparing for the all-round collectivization of agriculture, Bukharin pressed his erroneous view more openly than ever, endeavouring to cover up the class contradiction between the rich peasants and the poor and middle peasants and to oppose resolute struggle against the rich peasants. He also maintained the fallacy that the working class could form an alliance with the rich peasants who could "grow into socialism peacefully".

[11] V. I. Lenin, "On the Question of Dialectics", *Collected Works*, Russ. ed., Moscow, 1958, Vol. XXXVIII, pp. 358-59.

[12] See V. I. Lenin, " 'Communism' " (June 12, 1920), in which Lenin, criticizing the leader of the Hungarian Communist Party Bela Kun, said that he "gives up the most essential thing in Marxism, the living soul of Marxism, the concrete analysis of concrete conditions". (*Collected Works*, Russ. ed., Moscow, 1950, Vol. XXXI, p. 143.)

[13] Sun Wu Tzu, or Sun Wu, also known as Sun Tzu, was a famous Chinese soldier and military scientist in the 5th century B.C., who wrote *Sun Tzu*, a treatise on war containing thirteen chapters. This quotation is from Chapter 3, "The Strategy of Attack".

[14] Wei Cheng (A.D. 580-643) was a statesman and historian of the Tang Dynasty.

[15] *Shui Hu Chuan (Heroes of the Marshes)*, a famous 14th century Chinese novel, describes a peasant war towards the end of the Northern Sung Dynasty. Chu Village was in the vicinity of Liangshanpo, where Sung Chiang, leader of the peasant uprising and hero of the novel, established his base. Chu Chao-feng, the head of this village, was a despotic landlord.

[16] V. I. Lenin, "Once Again on the Trade Unions, the Present Situation and the Mistakes of Trotsky and Bukharin" (January 1921), *Selected Works*, Eng. ed., International Publishers, New York, 1943, Vol. IX, p. 66.

[17] The Revolution of 1911 was the bourgeois revolution which overthrew the autocratic regime of the Ching Dynasty. On October 10 of that year, a section of the Ching Dynasty's New Army who were under

revolutionary influence staged an uprising in Wuchang, Hupeh Province. The existing bourgeois and petty-bourgeois revolutionary societies and the broad masses of the workers, peasants and soldiers responded enthusiastically, and very soon the rule of the Ching Dynasty crumbled. In January 1912, the Provisional Government of the Republic of China was set up in Nanking, with Sun Yat-sen as the Provisional President. Thus China's feudal monarchic system which had lasted for more than two thousand years was brought to an end. The idea of a democratic republic had entered deep in the hearts of the people. But the bourgeoisie which led the revolution was strongly conciliationist in nature. It did not mobilize the peasant masses on an extensive scale to crush the feudal rule of the landlord class in the countryside, but instead handed state power over to the Northern warlord Yuan Shih-kai under imperialist and feudal pressure. As a result, the revolution ended in defeat.

18 The revolution of 1924-27, also known as the First Revolutionary Civil War, was an anti-imperialist and anti-feudal revolutionary struggle, whose main content was the Northern Expedition carried out on the basis of co-operation between the Chinese Communist Party and the Kuomintang. After consolidating its revolutionary base areas in Kwangtung Province, the revolutionary army which was established jointly by the two parties started its northward expedition against the imperialist-nurtured Northern warlords in July 1926 and won the warm support of the broad masses of workers and peasants. It occupied most of the provinces along the Yangtse and Yellow Rivers in the second half of 1926 and the first half of 1927. While the revolution was forging ahead successfully, the reactionary cliques within the Kuomintang headed by Chiang Kai-shek and by Wang Ching-wei (both representing the interests of the comprador and landlord classes) staged two counter-revolutionary coups d'état with the support of imperialism, the first in April 1927 and the second in July. The Rightist ideas then to be found in the Chinese Communist Party, which were represented by Chen Tu-hsiu, developed into a capitulationist line, so that the Party and the people were not in a position to organize effective resistance to the surprise attacks launched by the Kuomintang reactionary cliques, and the revolution suffered defeat.

19 The Agrarian Revolutionary War was the revolutionary struggle of the Chinese people waged under the leadership of the Communist Party from 1927 to 1937, and its main content consisted of the establishment and development of Red political power, the spread of the agrarian revolution and armed resistance to the rule of Kuomintang reaction. This revolutionary war is also known as the Second Revolutionary Civil War.

[20] The "four northeastern provinces" were then Liaoning, Kirin, Heilungkiang and Jehol, which correspond to the present Liaoning, Kirin and Heilungkiang Provinces, the northeastern part of Hopei Province north of the Great Wall and the eastern part of the Inner Mongolian Autonomous Region. After the September 18th Incident which took place in 1931, the Japanese invaders occupied Liaoning, Kirin and Heilungkiang and later, in 1933, seized Jehol.

[21] Under the influence of the Chinese Red Army and the people's anti-Japanese movement, the Kuomintang's Northeastern Army headed by Chang Hsueh-liang and the Kuomintang's 17th Route Army headed by Yang Hu-cheng accepted the policy of the anti-Japanese national united front proposed by the Communist Party of China, and demanded that Chiang Kai-shek should unite with the Communist Party to resist Japan. Chiang Kai-shek not only refused but became still more perverse and stepped up his military preparations for the "suppression of the Communists" and repressed the students' anti-Japanese movement in Sian. On December 12, 1936 Chang Hsueh-liang and Yang Hu-cheng staged the Sian Incident and arrested Chiang Kai-shek. After the occurrence of the incident, the Chinese Communist Party expressed firm support for Chang Hsueh-liang's and Yang Hu-cheng's patriotic action, and at the same time held that the incident should be settled on the basis of unity and resistance to Japan. On December 25 Chiang Kai-shek was compelled to accept the terms of unity with the Communist Party against Japan, and he was then set free and returned to Nanking.

[22] Chen Tu-hsiu was a radical democrat around the time of the May 4th Movement. Later, under the influence of the October Socialist Revolution he became one of the founders of the Chinese Communist Party. For six years after the founding of the Party he held the leading position in the Central Committee. His thinking had long been strongly Rightist. In the latter part of the 1924-27 revolution, it developed into a line of capitulationism. The capitulationists represented by Chen Tu-hsiu "voluntarily gave up the Party's leadership of the peasant masses, urban petty bourgeoisie and middle bourgeoisie, and in particular gave up the Party's leadership of the armed forces, thus causing the defeat of the revolution". ("The Present Situation and Our Tasks", *Selected Works of Mao Tse-tung*, Eng. ed., FLP, Peking, 1961, Vol. IV, p. 171.) After the defeat of 1927 Chen Tu-hsiu and a handful of other capitulationists lost faith in the future of the revolution and became liquidationists. They took a reactionary Trotskyite stand and formed a small anti-Party group together with the Trotskyites. Consequently Chen Tu-hsiu was expelled from the Party in November 1929. He died in 1942.

[23] For many decades, beginning with the end of the 18th century, Britain exported an increasing quantity of opium to China. This traffic not only subjected the Chinese people to drugging but also plundered China of her silver. It aroused fierce opposition in China. In 1840, under the pretext of safeguarding its trade with China, Britain launched armed aggression against her. The Chinese troops led by Lin Tse-hsu put up resistance, and the people in Canton spontaneously organized the "Quell-the-British Corps", which dealt serious blows to the British forces of aggression. In 1842, however, the corrupt Ching regime signed the Treaty of Nanking with the British aggressor. This treaty provided for the payment of indemnities and the cession of Hongkong to Britain, and stipulated that Shanghai, Foochow, Amoy, Ningpo and Canton were to be opened to British trade and that tariff rates for British goods imported into China were to be jointly fixed by China and Britain.

[24] The Sino-Japanese War of 1894 was started by Japanese imperialism for the purpose of invading Korea and China. Many Chinese soldiers and some patriotic generals put up a heroic fight. But China suffered defeat because of the corruption of the Ching government and its failure to prepare resistance. In 1895 the Ching government concluded the shameful Treaty of Shimonoseki with Japan.

[25] From Lenin's notes on "Determinateness (Quality)" in Hegel's *The Science of Logic*, Book I, Section 1. V. I. Lenin, "Conspectus of Hegel's *The Science of Logic*", *Collected Works*, Russ. ed., Moscow, 1958, Vol. XXXVIII, pp. 97-98.

[26] *Shan Hai Ching (Book of Mountains and Seas)* was written in the era of the Warring States (403-221 B.C.). In one of its fables Kua Fu, a superman, pursued and overtook the sun. But he died of thirst, whereupon his staff was transformed into the forest of Teng.

[27] Yi is one of the legendary heroes of ancient China, famous for his archery. According to a legend in *Huai Nan Tzu*, compiled in the 2nd century B.C., there were ten suns in the sky in the days of Emperor Yao. To put an end to the damage to vegetation caused by these scorching suns, Emperor Yao ordered Yi to shoot them down. In another legend recorded by Wang Yi (2nd century A.D.), the archer is said to have shot down nine of the ten suns.

[28] *Hsi Yu Chi (Pilgrimage to the West)* is a 16th century novel, the hero of which is the monkey god Sun Wu-kung. He could miraculously change at will into seventy-two different shapes, such as a bird, a tree and a stone.

[29] The *Strange Tales of Liao Chai*, written by Pu Sung-ling in the 17th century, is a well-known collection of 431 tales, mostly about ghosts and fox spirits.

[30] Karl Marx, "Introduction to the Critique of Political Economy", *A Contribution to the Critique of Political Economy*, Eng. ed., Chicago, 1904, pp. 310-11.

[31] The Paris Commune was the first proletarian organ of state power in world history. On March 18, 1871, the French proletariat launched an uprising in Paris and seized power. Led by the proletariat, the Paris Commune was founded on March 28 through election. It was the first revolutionary attempt of the proletariat to smash the bourgeois state machinery and an unprecedented feat to substitute proletarian state power for the bourgeois state power which had been overthrown. Not being mature enough at the time, the French proletariat failed to unite with its ally, the peasant masses, was too lenient to the counter-revolution and did not launch resolute military attacks in good time. Thus the counter-revolution could unhurriedly muster its routed forces, make a comeback and perpetrate a savage massacre of the people who took part in the uprising. The Paris Commune fell on May 28.

[32] V. I. Lenin, "On the Question of Dialectics", *Collected Works*, Russ. ed., Moscow, 1958, Vol. XXXVIII, p. 358.

[33] The saying "Things that oppose each other also complement each other" first appeared in the *History of the Earlier Han Dynasty* by Pan Ku, a celebrated historian in the 1st century A.D. It has long been a popular saying.

[34] V. I. Lenin, "On the Question of Dialectics", *Collected Works*, Russ. ed., Moscow, 1958, Vol. XXXVIII, p. 358.

[35] Trotsky (1879-1940) headed an anti-Leninist faction in the Russian revolutionary movement and later degenerated and joined the gang of counter-revolution. He was expelled from the Party by the Central Committee of the CPSU in 1927, banished by the Soviet government in 1929 and deprived of Soviet nationality in 1932.

[36] V. I. Lenin, "Remarks on N. I. Bukharin's *Economics of the Transitional Period*", *Selected Works*, Russ. ed., Moscow-Leningrad, 1931, Vol. XI, p. 357.

ON THE CORRECT HANDLING
OF CONTRADICTIONS
AMONG THE PEOPLE

February 27, 1957

Our general subject is the correct handling of contradictions among the people. For the sake of convenience, let us discuss it under twelve sub-headings. Although reference will be made to contradictions between ourselves and the enemy, this discussion will centre mainly on contradictions among the people.

I. TWO DIFFERENT TYPES OF CONTRADICTIONS

Never before has our country been as united as it is today. The victories of the bourgeois-democratic revolution and the socialist revolution and our achievements in socialist construction have rapidly changed the face of old China. A still brighter future for our motherland lies ahead. The days of national disunity and chaos which the people detested have

---

This is the text of a speech made at the Eleventh Session (Enlarged) of the Supreme State Conference. The author went over the verbatim record and made certain additions before its publication in *Renmin Ribao (People's Daily)* on June 19 of the same year.

gone, never to return. Led by the working class and the Communist Party, our six hundred million people, united as one, are engaged in the great task of building socialism. The unification of our country, the unity of our people and the unity of our various nationalities — these are the basic guarantees of the sure triumph of our cause. However, this does not mean that contradictions no longer exist in our society. To imagine that none exist is a naive idea which is at variance with objective reality. We are confronted by two types of social contradictions — those between ourselves and the enemy and those among the people themselves. The two are totally different in their nature.

To understand these two different types of contradictions correctly, we must first be clear on what is meant by "the people" and what is meant by "the enemy". The concept of "the people" varies in content in different countries and in different periods of history in the same country. Take our own country for example. During the War of Resistance Against Japan, all those classes, strata and social groups opposing Japanese aggression came within the category of the people, while the Japanese imperialists, the Chinese traitors and the pro-Japanese elements were all enemies of the people. During the War of Liberation, the U.S. imperialists and their running dogs — the bureaucrat-capitalists, the landlords and the Kuomintang reactionaries who represented these two classes — were the enemies of the people, while the other classes, strata and social groups, which opposed these enemies, all came within the category of the people. At the present stage, the period of building socialism, the classes, strata and social groups which favour, support and work for the cause of socialist construction all come within the category of the people, while the social forces and groups which resist the socialist revolution and are hostile to or sabotage socialist construction are enemies of the people.

The contradictions between ourselves and the enemy are antagonistic contradictions. Within the ranks of our people, the contradictions among the working people are non-antagonistic, while those between the exploited and the exploiting classes have a non-antagonistic aspect in addition to an antagonistic aspect. There have always been contradictions among the people, but their content differs in each period of the revolution and in the period of socialist construction. In the conditions prevailing in China today, the contradictions among the people comprise the contradictions within the working class, the contradictions within the peasantry, the contradictions within the intelligentsia, the contradictions between the working class and the peasantry, the contradictions between the workers and peasants on the one hand and the intellectuals on the other, the contradictions between the working class and other sections of the working people on the one hand and the national bourgeoisie on the other, the contradictions within the national bourgeoisie, and so on. Our People's Government is one that genuinely represents the people's interests, it is a government that serves the people. Nevertheless, there are still certain contradictions between the government and the people. These include contradictions among the interests of the state, the interests of the collective and the interests of the individual; between democracy and centralism; between the leadership and the led; and the contradiction arising from the bureaucratic style of work of certain government workers in their relations with the masses. All these are also contradictions among the people. Generally speaking, the people's basic identity of interests underlies the contradictions among the people.

In our country, the contradiction between the working class and the national bourgeoisie belongs to the category of contradictions among the people. By and large, the class struggle between the two is a class struggle within the ranks of the people, because the Chinese national bourgeoisie has a dual character. In the period of the bourgeois-democratic revolution, it had a revolutionary as well as a conciliationist side to its character. In the period of the socialist revolution, exploitation of the working class for profit constitutes one side of the character of the national bourgeoisie, while its support of the Constitution and its willingness to accept socialist transformation constitute the other. The national bourgeoisie differs from the imperialists, the landlords and the bureaucrat-capitalists. The contradiction between the national bourgeoisie and the working class is one between the exploiter and the exploited, and is therefore antagonistic in nature. But in the concrete conditions of China, this antagonistic class contradiction can, if properly handled, be transformed into a non-antagonistic one and be resolved by peaceful methods. However, it can change into a contradiction between ourselves and the enemy if we do not handle it properly and do not follow the policy of uniting with, criticizing and educating the national bourgeoisie, or if the national bourgeoisie does not accept this policy of ours.

Since they are different in nature, the contradictions between ourselves and the enemy and the contradictions among the people must be resolved by different methods. To put it briefly, the former are a matter of drawing a clear distinction between ourselves and the enemy, and the latter a matter of drawing a clear distinction between right and wrong. It is, of course, true that the distinction between ourselves and the enemy is also a matter of right and wrong. For example, the question of who is in the right, we or the domestic and foreign reactionaries, the imperialists, the feudalists and bureaucrat-capitalists, is also a matter of right and wrong, but it is in a different category from questions of right and wrong among the people.

Our state is a people's democratic dictatorship led by the working class and based on the worker-peasant alliance. What is this dictatorship for? Its first function is to suppress the reactionary classes and elements and those exploiters in our country who range themselves against the socialist revolution, to suppress all those who try to wreck our socialist construction, or in other words, to resolve the internal contradictions between ourselves and the enemy. For instance, to arrest, try and sentence certain counter-revolutionaries, and to deprive landlords and bureaucrat-capitalists of their right to vote and their freedom of speech for a specified period of time — all this comes within the scope of our dictatorship. To maintain public order and safeguard the interests of the people, it is likewise necessary to exercise dictatorship over embezzlers, swindlers, arsonists, murderers, criminal gangs and other scoundrels who seriously disrupt public order. The second function of this dictatorship is to protect our country from subversion and possible aggression by external enemies. In that event, it is the task of this dictatorship to resolve the external contradiction between ourselves and the enemy. The aim of this dictatorship is to protect all our people so that they can devote themselves to peaceful labour and build China into a socialist country with a modern industry, agriculture, science and culture. Who is to exercise this dictatorship? Naturally, the working class and the entire people under its leadership. Dictatorship does not apply within the ranks of the people. The people cannot exercise dictatorship over themselves, nor must one section of the people oppress another. Law-breaking elements among the people will be punished according to law, but this is different in principle from the exercise of dictatorship to suppress enemies of the people. What applies among the people is democratic centralism. Our Constitution lays it down that citizens of the People's Republic of China enjoy freedom of speech, of the press, assembly, association, procession, demonstration, religious belief, and so on. Our Constitution also provides that the organs of state must practise democratic centralism, that they must rely on the masses and that their personnel must serve the people. Our socialist democracy is democracy in the broadest sense such as is not to be found in any capitalist country. Our dictatorship is the people's democratic dictatorship led by the working class and based on the worker-peasant alliance. That is to say, democracy operates within the ranks of the people, while the working class, uniting with all others enjoying civil rights, and in the first place with the peasantry, enforces dictatorship over the reactionary classes and elements and all those who resist socialist transformation and oppose socialist construction. By civil rights, we mean, politically, the rights of freedom and democracy.

But this freedom is freedom with leadership and this democracy is democracy under centralized guidance, not anarchy. Anarchy does not accord with the interests or wishes of the people.

Certain people in our country were delighted by the events in Hungary.[1] They hoped that something similar would happen in China, that thousands upon thousands of people would demonstrate in the streets against the People's Government. Their hopes ran counter to the interests of the masses and therefore could not possibly win their support. Deceived by domestic and foreign counter-revolutionaries, a section of the people in Hungary made the mistake of resorting to acts of violence against the People's Government, with the result that both the state and the people suffered. The damage done to the country's economy in a few weeks of rioting will take a long time to repair. There are other people in our country who wavered on the question of the Hungarian events because they were ignorant of the real state of affairs in the world. They think that there is too little freedom under our people's democracy and that there is more freedom under Western parliamentary democracy. They ask for a two-party system as in the West, with one party in office and the other out of office. But this so-called two-party system is nothing but a device for maintaining the dictatorship of the bourgeoisie; it can never guarantee freedom to the working people. As a matter of fact, freedom and democracy do not exist in the abstract, only in the concrete. In a society rent by class struggle, if there is freedom for the exploiting classes to exploit the working people, there is no freedom for the working people not to be exploited, and if there is democracy for the bourgeoisie, there is no democracy for the proletariat and other working people. The legal existence of the Communist Party is tolerated in some capitalist countries, but only to the extent that it does not endanger the fundamental interests of the bourgeoisie; it is not tolerated beyond that. Those who demand freedom and democracy in the abstract regard democracy as an end and not a means. Democracy sometimes seems to be an end, but it is in fact only a means. Marxism teaches us that democracy is part of the superstructure and belongs to the category of politics. That is to say, in the last analysis, it serves the economic base. The same is true of freedom. Both democracy and freedom are relative, not absolute, and they come into being and develop in specific historical conditions. Within the ranks of the people, democracy is correlative with centralism, and freedom with discipline. They are the two opposites of a single entity, contradictory as well as united, and we should not one-sidedly emphasize one to the denial of the other. Within the ranks of the people, we cannot do without freedom, nor can we do without discipline; we cannot do without democracy, nor can we do without centralism. This unity of democracy and centralism, of freedom and discipline, constitutes our democratic centralism. Under this system, the people enjoy extensive democracy and freedom, but at the same time they have to keep within the bounds of socialist discipline. All this is well understood by the broad masses of the people.

In advocating freedom with leadership and democracy under centralized guidance, we in no way mean that coercive measures should be taken to settle ideological questions or questions involving the distinction between right and wrong among the people. All attempts to use administrative orders or coercive measures to settle ideological questions or questions of right and wrong are not only ineffective but harmful. We cannot abolish religion by administrative decree or force people not to believe in it. We cannot compel people to give up idealism, any more than we can force them to believe in Marxism. The only way to settle questions of an ideological nature or controversial issues among the people is by the democratic method, the method of discussion, of criticism, of persuasion and education, and not by the method of coercion or repression. To be able to carry on their production and studies effectively and to arrange their lives properly, the people want their government and those in charge of production and of cultural and educational organizations to issue appropriate orders of an obligatory nature. It is common sense that the maintenance of public order would be impossible without such administrative regulations. Administrative orders and the method of persuasion and education complement each other in resolving contradictions among the people. Even administrative regulations for the maintenance of public order must be accompanied by persuasion and education, for in many cases regulations alone will not work.

This democratic method of resolving contradictions among the people was epitomized in 1942 in the formula "unity, criticism, unity". To elaborate, it means starting from the desire for unity, resolving contradictions through criticism or struggle and arriving at a new unity on a new basis. In our experience this is the correct method of resolving contradictions among the people. In 1942 we used it to resolve contradictions inside the Communist Party, namely, the contradictions between the dogmatists and the great majority of the membership, and between dogmatism and Marxism. The "Left" dogmatists had resorted to the method of "ruthless struggle and merciless blows" in inner-Party struggle. This method was incorrect. In criticizing "Left" dogmatism, we discarded this old method and adopted a new one, that is, one of starting from the desire for unity, distinguishing between right and wrong through criticism or struggle and arriving at a new unity on a new basis. This was the method used in the rectification movement of 1942. Thus within a few years, by the time the Chinese Communist Party held its Seventh National Congress in 1945, unity was achieved throughout the Party, and as a consequence the great victory of the people's revolution was won. The essential thing is to start from the desire for unity. For without this desire for unity, the struggle is certain to get out of hand. Wouldn't this be the same as "ruthless struggle and merciless blows"? And what Party unity would there be left? It was this very experience that led us to the formula: "unity, criticism, unity." Or, in other words, "learn from past mistakes to avoid future ones and cure the sickness to save the patient". We extended this method beyond our Party. We applied it with great success in the anti-Japanese base areas in dealing with the relations between the leadership and the masses, between the army and the people, between officers and men, between the different units of the army, and between the different groups of cadres. The use of this method can be traced back to still earlier times in our Party's history. It has been used ever since the building of our revolutionary armed forces and base areas in the south in 1927 to deal with the relations between the Party and the masses, between the army and the people, between officers and men, and other relations among the people. The only difference is that during the anti-Japanese war, we employed this method with much greater consciousness of purpose. And since the liberation of the whole country, we have employed this same method of "unity, criticism, unity" in our relations with the democratic parties and with industrial and commercial circles. Our task now is to continue to extend and make still better use of this method throughout the ranks of the people; we want all our factories, co-operatives, business establishments, schools, government offices and public organizations, in a word, all our six hundred million people, to use it in resolving contradictions among ourselves.

In ordinary circumstances, contradictions among the people are not antagonistic. But if they are not handled properly, or if we relax our vigilance and lower our guard, antagonism may arise. In a socialist country, a development of this kind is usually only a localized and temporary phenomenon. The reason is that the system of exploitation of man by man has been abolished and the interests of the people are basically the same. The antagonistic actions which took place on a fairly wide scale during the Hungarian events were the result of the operations of both domestic and foreign counter-revolutionary elements. This, too, was a temporary, though special, phenomenon. It was a case of reactionaries inside a socialist country, in league with the imperialists, attempting to achieve their conspiratorial aims by taking advantage of contradictions among the people to foment dissension and stir up disorder. This lesson of the Hungarian events merits attention.

Many people seem to think that the question of using democratic methods to resolve contradictions among the people is a new one. Actually it is not. Marxists have always held that the cause of the proletariat must depend on the masses of the people and that Communists must use the democratic method of persuasion and education when working among the labouring people and must on no account resort to commandism or coercion. The Chinese Communist Party faithfully adheres to this Marxist-Leninist principle. It has been our consistent view that, under the people's democratic dictatorship, two different methods, one dictatorial and the other democratic, should be used to resolve the two different kinds of contradictions — those between ourselves and the enemy and those among the people. This idea has been explained again and again in our Party documents and in speeches by many responsible Party leaders. In my article "On the People's Democratic Dictatorship" written in 1949, I said, "The combination of these two aspects, democracy for the people and dictatorship over the reactionaries, is the people's democratic dictatorship." I also pointed out that, in order to settle problems within the ranks of the people, "the method we employ is democratic, the method of persuasion, not of compulsion". Again, in addressing the Second Session of the National Committee of the People's Political Consultative Conference in June 1950, I said:

The people's democratic dictatorship uses two methods. In regard to the enemy, it uses the method of dictatorship, in other words, it forbids them to take part in political activity for as long a period of time as is necessary and it compels them to obey the laws of the People's Government, to work and to transform themselves into new people through labour. In regard to the people, on the contrary, it uses not the compulsory but the democratic method, in other words, it allows the people to take part in political activities and uses the democratic method of education and persuasion instead of compelling them to do this or that. This education is self-education within the ranks of the people, and the basic method of self-education is criticism and self-criticism.

Thus, on many occasions we have discussed the use of the democratic method for resolving contradictions among the people; furthermore, we have in the main applied it in our work, and many cadres and many other people are familiar with it in practice. Why then do some people now feel that it is a new issue? Because, in the past, the struggle between ourselves and the enemy, both internal and external, was most acute, and contradictions among the people therefore did not attract as much attention as they do today.

Quite a few people fail to make a clear distinction between these two different types of contradictions — those between ourselves and the enemy and those among the people — and are prone to confuse the two. It must be admitted that it is sometimes quite easy to do so. We have had instances of such confusion in our work in the past. In the course of suppressing counter-revolutionaries, good people were sometimes mistaken for bad, and such things still happen today. We are able to keep our mistakes within bounds because it has been our policy to draw a sharp line between ourselves and the enemy and to rectify mistakes whenever discovered.

Marxist philosophy holds that the law of the unity of opposites is the fundamental law of the universe. This law operates universally, whether in the natural world, in human society, or in man's thinking. Between the opposites in a contradiction there is at once unity and struggle, and it is this that impels things to move and change. Contradictions exist everywhere, but they differ in accordance with the different nature of different things. In any given phenomenon or thing, the unity of opposites is conditional, temporary and transitory, and hence relative, whereas the struggle of opposites is absolute. Lenin gave a very clear exposition of this law. In our country, a growing number of people have come to understand it. For many people, however, acceptance of this law is one thing, and its application in examining and dealing with problems is quite another. Many dare not openly admit that contradictions still exist among the people of our country, although it is these very contradictions that are pushing our society forward. Many do not admit that contradictions continue to exist in a socialist society, with the result that they are handicapped and passive when confronted with social contradictions; they do not understand that socialist society will grow more united and consolidated through the ceaseless process of the correct handling and resolving of contradictions. For this reason, we need to explain things to our people, and to our cadres in the first place, in order to help them understand the contradictions in a socialist society and learn to use correct methods for handling these contradictions.

Contradictions in a socialist society are fundamentally different from those in the old societies, such as capitalist society. In capitalist society contradictions find expression in acute antagonisms and conflicts, in sharp class struggle; they cannot be resolved by the capitalist system itself and can only be resolved by socialist revolution. On the contrary, the case is different with contradictions in socialist society, where they are not antagonistic and can be resolved one after another by the socialist system itself.

The basic contradictions in socialist society are still those between the relations of production and the productive forces and between the superstructure and the economic base. However, they are fundamentally different in character and have different features from the contradictions between the relations of production and the productive forces and between the superstructure and the economic base in the old societies. The present social system of our country is far superior to that of the old days. If it were not so, the old system would not have been overthrown and the new system could not have been established. In saying that socialist relations of production are better suited to the development of the productive forces than are the old relations of production, we mean that they permit the productive forces to develop at a speed unattainable in the old society, so that production can expand steadily to meet the constantly growing needs of the people step by step. Under the rule of imperialism, feudalism and bureaucrat-capitalism, the productive forces of old China developed very slowly. For more than fifty years before liberation, China produced only a few tens of thousands of tons of steel a year, not counting the output of the northeastern provinces. If these provinces are included, the peak annual steel output only amounted to just over 900,000 tons. In 1949, national steel output was only a little over 100,000 tons. Yet now, a mere seven years after the liberation of our country, steel output already exceeds four million tons. In old China, there was hardly any machine-building industry, to say nothing of automobile and aviation industries; now, we have all three. When the people overthrew the rule of imperialism, feudalism and bureaucrat-capitalism, many were not clear as to which way China should head — towards capitalism or towards socialism. Facts have now provided the answer: only socialism can save China. The socialist system has promoted the rapid development of the productive forces of our country; this is a fact even our enemies abroad have had to acknowledge.

But our socialist system has only just been set up; it is not yet fully established or fully consolidated. In joint state-private industrial and commercial enterprises, capitalists still receive a fixed rate of interest on their capital,[2] that is to say, exploitation still exists. So far as ownership is concerned, these enterprises are not yet completely socialist in character. Some of our agricultural and handicraft producers' co-operatives are still semi-socialist, while even in the fully socialist co-operatives certain problems of ownership remain to be solved. Relations between production and exchange in accordance with socialist principles are still being gradually established in various departments of our economy, and more and more appropriate forms are being sought. To decide the proper ratio between accumulation and consumption within each of the two sectors of socialist economy — that in which the means of production are owned by the whole people and that in which the means of production are collectively owned — and also between the two sectors themselves is a complicated problem for which it is not easy to work out a perfectly rational solution all at once. To sum up, socialist relations of production have been established and are in harmony with the growth of the productive forces, but they are still far from perfect, and this imperfection stands in contradiction to the growth of the productive forces. Apart from harmony as well as contradiction between the relations of production and the developing productive forces, there is harmony as well as contradiction between the superstructure and the economic base. The superstructure consisting of the state system and laws of the people's democratic dictatorship and the socialist ideology guided by Marxism-Leninism plays a positive role in facilitating the victory of socialist transformation and the establishment of the socialist organization of labour; it is suited to the socialist economic base, that is, to socialist relations of production. But survivals of bourgeois ideology, certain bureaucratic ways of doing things in our state organs and defects in certain links in our state institutions are in contradiction with the socialist economic base. We must continue to resolve all such contradictions in the light of our specific conditions. Of course, new problems will emerge as these contradictions are resolved. And further efforts will be required to resolve the new contradictions. For instance, a constant process of readjustment through state planning is needed to deal with the contradiction between production and the needs of society, which will long remain as an objective reality. Every year our country draws up an economic plan in order to establish a proper ratio between accumulation and consumption and achieve a balance between production and needs. Balance is nothing but a temporary, relative unity of opposites. By the end of each year, this balance, taken as a whole, is upset by the struggle of opposites; the unity undergoes a change, balance becomes imbalance, unity becomes disunity, and once again it is necessary to work out a balance and unity for the next year. Herein lies the superiority of our planned economy. As a matter of fact, this balance, this unity, is partially upset every month or every quarter, and partial readjustments are called for. Sometimes, contradictions arise and the balance is upset because our subjective arrangements do not correspond to objective reality; this is what we call making a mistake. The ceaseless emergence and ceaseless resolution of contradictions is the dialectical law of the development of things.

Today, matters stand as follows. The large-scale and turbulent class struggles of the masses characteristic of the previous revolutionary periods have in the main ended, but class struggle is by no means entirely over. While welcoming the new system, the broad masses of the people are not yet quite accustomed to it. Government workers are not sufficiently experienced and have to undertake further study and exploration of specific policies. In other words, time is needed for our socialist system to become established and consolidated, for the masses to become accustomed to the new system, and for the government workers to learn and acquire experience. It is therefore imperative at this juncture that we should raise the question of distinguishing contradictions among the people from those between ourselves and the enemy, as well as the question of the correct handling of contradictions among the people, so as to unite the people of all nationalities in our country for a new battle, the battle against nature, to develop our economy and culture, to help the whole nation to traverse this period of transition fairly smoothly, to consolidate our new system and build up our new state.

II. THE QUESTION OF THE SUPPRESSION OF COUNTER-REVOLUTIONARIES

The question of suppressing counter-revolutionaries is one of struggle between ourselves and the enemy, an antagonistic contradiction. Among the people, there are some who see this question in a somewhat different light. Two kinds of persons hold views different from ours. Those with a Rightist way of thinking make no distinction between ourselves and the enemy and take the enemy for our own people. They regard as friends the very persons whom the broad masses regard as enemies. Those with a "Left" way of thinking magnify contradictions between ourselves and the enemy to such an extent that they take certain contradictions among the people for contradictions with the enemy, and regard as counter-revolutionaries persons who are not really counter-revolutionaries. Both these views are wrong. Neither can lead to the correct handling of the question of suppressing counter-revolutionaries or to a correct assessment of this work.

To form a correct evaluation of our work in suppressing counter-revolutionaries, let us see what effect the Hungarian events have had in China. After their occurrence there was some unrest among a section of our intellectuals, but there were no squalls. Why? One reason, it must be said, is that we had succeeded in suppressing the counter-revolutionaries quite thoroughly.

Of course, the consolidation of our state is not primarily due to the suppression of counter-revolution. It is due primarily to the fact that we have a Communist Party, a Liberation Army and a working people tempered in decades of revolutionary struggle. Our Party and our armed forces are rooted in the masses; they have been tempered in the flames of a protracted revolution; they have the capacity to fight. Our People's Republic was not built overnight, but developed step by step out of the revolutionary base areas. Some democratic personages have also been tempered in the struggle in varying degrees, and they have gone through troubled times together with us. Some intellectuals were tempered in the struggles against imperialism and reaction; since liberation many of them have gone through a process of ideological remoulding aimed at enabling them to distinguish clearly between ourselves and the enemy. In addition, the consolidation of our state is due to the fact that our economic measures are basically sound, that the people's livelihood is secure and is steadily improving, that our policies towards the national bourgeoisie and other classes are correct, and so on. Nevertheless, our success in suppressing counter-revolutionaries is undoubtedly an important reason for the consolidation of our state. For all these reasons, with few exceptions our college students are patriotic and support socialism, although many of them come from other

97

than working class families; they did not give way to unrest during the Hungarian events. The same was true of the national bourgeoisie, to say nothing of the basic masses — the workers and peasants.

After liberation, we rooted out a number of counter-revolutionaries. Some were sentenced to death for major crimes. This was absolutely necessary, it was the demand of the people, it was done to free the masses from long years of oppression by the counter-revolutionaries and all kinds of local tyrants; in other words, it was done to release the productive forces. If we had not done so, the masses would not have been able to lift their heads. Since 1956, however, there has been a radical change in the situation. In the country as a whole, the bulk of the counter-revolutionaries have been cleared out. Our basic task has changed from unfettering the productive forces to protecting and expanding them in the context of the new relations of production. Because of their failure to understand that our present policy fits the present situation and our past policy fitted the past situation, some people want to make use of the present policy to reverse decisions on past cases and to deny the great success we achieved in suppressing counter-revolution. This is quite wrong, and the masses will not permit it.

Successes were the main thing in our work of suppressing counter-revolutionaries, but there were also mistakes. In some cases there were excesses and in others counter-revolutionaries slipped through our net. Our policy is: "Counter-revolutionaries must be suppressed wherever found, mistakes must be corrected whenever discovered." Our line in the work of suppressing counter-revolution is the mass line. Of course, even with the mass line mistakes may still occur in our work, but they will be fewer and easier to correct. The masses gain experience through struggle. From what is done correctly they learn how things should be done. From what is done wrong they learn useful lessons as to how mistakes should be avoided.

Wherever mistakes have been discovered in the work of suppressing counter-revolutionaries, steps have been or are being taken to correct them. Those not yet discovered will be corrected as soon as they come to light. Decisions on exoneration or rehabilitation should be made known as widely as were the original wrong decisions. I propose that a comprehensive review of the work of suppressing counter-revolutionaries be made this year or next to sum up experience and encourage standing up for what is right and combating what is evil.[3] Nationally, this review should be in the charge of the Standing Committee of the National People's Congress and the Standing Committee of the People's Political Consultative Conference, and locally, in the charge of the provincial and municipal people's councils and the committees of the People's Political Consultative Conference. In this review, we must help the large numbers of cadres and activists involved in the work, and not pour cold water on them. It would not be right to dampen their spirits. Nonetheless, wrongs must be righted when they are discovered. This must be the attitude of all the public security organs, the procurators' offices and the judicial departments, prisons and agencies charged with the reform of criminals through labour. We hope that wherever possible members of the Standing Committee of the National People's Congress and of the People's Political Consultative Conference and the people's deputies will take part in this review. This will be of help in perfecting our legal system and in dealing correctly with counter-revolutionaries and other criminals.

The present situation with regard to counter-revolutionaries can be described in these words: There still are counter-revolutionaries, but not many. In the first place, there still are counter-revolutionaries. Some people say that there aren't any more and all is at peace and that we can therefore lay our heads on our pillows and just drop off to sleep. But this is not the way things are. The fact is, there still are counter-revolutionaries (of course, that is not to say you'll find them everywhere and in every organization), and we must continue to fight them. It must be understood that the hidden counter-revolutionaries still at large will not take things lying down, but will certainly seize every opportunity to make trouble. The U.S. imperialists and the Chiang Kai-shek clique are constantly sending in secret agents to carry on disruptive activities. Even after all the existing counter-revolutionaries have been combed out, new ones may emerge. If we drop our guard, we shall be badly fooled and shall suffer severely. Counter-revolutionaries must be rooted out with a firm hand wherever they are found making trouble. But, taking the country as a whole, there are certainly not many counter-revolutionaries. It would be wrong to say that there are still large numbers of counter-revolutionaries in China. Acceptance of that view would also end up in a mess.

III. THE QUESTION OF AGRICULTURAL CO-OPERATION

We have a rural population of over five hundred million, so the situation of our peasants has a most important bearing on the development of our economy and the consolidation of our state power. In my view, the situation is basically sound. Agricultural co-operatives have been successfully organized, and this has resolved the great contradiction in our country between socialist industrialization and individual peasant farming. As the co-operative transformation of agriculture was completed so rapidly, some people were worried and wondered whether something untoward might occur. There are indeed some faults but, fortunately, they are not serious, and on the whole the movement is healthy. The peasants are working with a will and last year, despite the worst floods, droughts and typhoons in years, there was an increase in grain output. Now there are people who are stirring up a miniature typhoon: they are grousing that co-operative farming is no good, that it is not superior to individual farming. Is agricultural co-operation superior or not? Among the documents distributed at today's meeting is one about the Wang Kuo-fan Co-operative[4] in Tsunhua County, Hopei Province, which I suggest you read. This co-operative is situated in a hilly region which was very poor in the past and which for a number of years depended on relief grain from the People's Government. When the co-operative was first set up in 1953, people called it the "paupers' co-op". But it has become better off year by year, and now, after four years of hard struggle, most of its households have reserves of grain. What this co-operative could do, other co-operatives should also be able to do under normal conditions in the same period or slightly longer. Clearly then there are no grounds for saying that something has gone wrong with agricultural co-operation.

It is also clear that it takes hard struggle to build up co-operatives. New things always have to overcome difficulties and setbacks as they grow. It is sheer fantasy to imagine that building socialism is all plain sailing and easy success, without difficulties and setbacks or the exertion of tremendous efforts.

Who are the active supporters of the co-operatives? The overwhelming majority of the poor peasants and lower middle peasants, who account for more than 70 per cent of the rural population. Most of the rest are also hopeful about the co-operatives. Only a very small minority are really dissatisfied. Failing to analyse this situation, quite a number of persons have taken part of the picture for the whole, without making an overall examination of the achievements and shortcomings of the co-operatives and the causes of these shortcomings; thus a miniature typhoon has started up among some people, who argue that the co-operatives are not superior.

How long will it take to consolidate the co-operatives or end these arguments about their not being superior? Judging from the experience of many co-operatives, it will probably take five years or a little longer. As most of our co-operatives are only a little over a year old, it would be unreasonable to ask too much of them. In my view, we will be doing well enough if the co-operatives can be consolidated during the Second Five-Year Plan after being established in the First.

The co-operatives are now in the process of gradual consolidation. Certain contradictions remain to be resolved, such as those between the state and the co-operatives and those among and within the co-operatives themselves.

We must give constant attention to problems of production and distribution as the way to resolve these contradictions. Take the question of production. The co-operative economy must be subject to the unified economic planning of the state, while retaining a certain leeway and independence of action that are not incompatible with the state's unified plan or with its policies, laws and regulations. At the same time, every household in a co-operative must comply with the overall plan of the co-operative or production team to which it belongs, apart from any appropriate plans it makes for itself in regard to land allotted for private use and to other economic undertakings left to private management. On the question of the distribution of income, we must take account of the interests of the state, the collective and the individual. We must properly handle the three-way relationship between the state agricultural tax, the co-operative's accumulation fund and the peasants' personal income, and take constant care to make readjustments so as to resolve contradictions between them. Accumulation is essential both for the state and for the co-operative, but in neither case should it be excessive. We should do everything possible to enable the peasants to raise their personal incomes year by year in normal years on the basis of increased production.

Many people say that the peasants lead a hard life. Is this true? In one sense it is. That is to say, because the imperialists and their agents oppressed and exploited us for over a century, ours is an impoverished country and the standard of living not only of our peasants but of our workers and intellectuals is still low. We will need several decades of intensive effort to raise the standard of living of our entire people step by step. In this sense, "hard" is the right word. But in another sense, it is not true. We refer to the allegation that, in the seven years since liberation, improvements have taken place only in the life of the workers and not in that of the peasants. As a matter of fact, with very few exceptions, there has been some improvement in the peasants' life as well as in that of the workers. Since liberation, the peasants have been free from landlord exploitation and their production has increased year by year. Take grain crops. In 1949, the country's output was only something over 210,000 million catties. By 1956, it had risen to something over 360,000 million catties, an increase of nearly 150,000 million catties. The state agricultural tax is not heavy, only amounting to some 30,000 million catties a year. State purchases of grain from the peasants at standard prices only amount to something over 50,000 million catties a year. These two items together total over 80,000 million catties. Furthermore, more than half this grain is sold back to the villages and nearby towns. Obviously no one can say that there has been no improvement in the life of the peasants. We are preparing to stabilize the total annual amount of the grain tax plus the grain purchased by the state at approximately 80,000 million catties in the next few years, so as to help agriculture to develop and the co-operatives to become consolidated. In this way, the small number of grain-deficient households still found in the countryside will cease to go short, and all peasant households, with the exception of some growing industrial crops, will have grain reserves or at least become self-sufficient; there will be no more poor peasants and the standard of living of the entire peasantry will reach or surpass the middle peasant level. It is not right simply to compare a peasant's average annual income with a worker's and draw the conclusion that one is too low and the other too high. The productivity of the workers is much higher than that of the peasants, while the latter's cost of living is much lower than that of workers in the cities, so the workers cannot be said to have received special favours from the state. However, the wages of a small number of workers and some government personnel are a bit too high, and the peasants have reason to be dissatisfied with this, so it is necessary to make certain appropriate readjustments according to specific circumstances.

IV. THE QUESTION OF INDUSTRIALISTS AND MERCHANTS

With regard to the transformation of our social system, the year 1956 saw the conversion of privately owned industrial and commercial enterprises into joint state-private enterprises, in addition to the organization of co-operatives in agriculture and handicrafts. The speed and smoothness of this conversion were closely related to our treatment of the contradiction between the working class and the national bourgeoisie as a contradiction among the people. Has this class contradiction been completely resolved? No, not yet. That will still take a considerable period of time. However, some people say the capitalists have been so remoulded that they are now not much different from the workers and that further remoulding is unnecessary. Others go so far as to say that the capitalists are now even a little better than the workers. Still others ask, if remoulding is necessary, why doesn't the working class undergo remoulding? Are these opinions correct? Of course not.

In the building of a socialist society, everybody needs remoulding — the exploiters and also the working people. Who says the working class does not need it? Of course, the remoulding of the exploiters is qualitatively different from that of the working people, and the two must not be confused. The working class remoulds the whole of society in class struggle and in the struggle against nature, and at the same time remoulds itself. It must ceaselessly learn in the course of its work and overcome its shortcomings step by step, and must never stop doing so. Take those of us who are present here for example. Many of us make some progress each year; that is to say, we are being re-moulded each year. For myself, I had all sorts of non-Marxist ideas before, and it was only later that I embraced Marxism. I learned a little Marxism from books and so made an initial remoulding of my ideas, but it was mainly through taking part in the class struggle over the years that I came to be remoulded. And I must continue to learn if I am to make further progress, or otherwise I shall lag behind. Can the capitalists be so good that they need no more remoulding?

Some people contend that the Chinese bourgeoisie no longer has two sides to its character, but only one side. Is this true? No. While members of the bourgeoisie have become administrative personnel in joint state-private enterprises and are being transformed from exploiters into working people living by their own labour, they still receive a fixed rate of interest on their share of capital in the joint enterprises, that is, they have not yet cut themselves loose from the roots of exploitation. Between them and the working class there is still a considerable gap in ideology, sentiments and habits of life. How is it possible to say that they no longer have two sides to their character? Even when they stop receiving their fixed interest payments and the "bourgeois" label is removed, they will still need ideo-logical remoulding for quite some time. If the bourgeoisie no longer had a dual character as these people maintain, then the capitalists would no longer have the task of studying and of remoulding themselves.

It must be said that this view does not tally either with the actual situation of our industrialists and merchants or with what most of them want. During the past few years, most of them have been willing to study and have made marked progress. Their thorough remoulding can be achieved only in the course of work; they should work together with the staff and workers in the enterprises, and regard the enterprises as the chief places in which to remould themselves. But it is also important for them to change some of their old views through study. Such study should be on a voluntary basis. When they return to the enterprises after attending study groups for some weeks, many industrialists and merchants find that they have more of a common language with the workers and representatives of the state shareholdings, and so there are better possibilities for working together. They know from personal experience that it is good for them to keep on studying and remoulding themselves. The idea that study and remoulding are not necessary reflects the views not of the majority of industrialists and merchants but only of a small number.

V. THE QUESTION OF THE INTELLECTUALS

The contradictions within the ranks of the people in our country also find expression among the intellectuals. The several million intellectuals who worked for the old society have come to serve the new society, and the question that now arises is how they can fit in with the needs of the new society and how we can help them to do so. This, too, is a contradiction among the people.

Most of our intellectuals have made marked progress during the last seven years. They have expressed themselves in favour of the socialist system. Many are diligently studying Marxism, and some have become communists. The latter, though small in number, are steadily growing. Of course, there are still some intellectuals who are sceptical about socialism or who do not approve of it, but they are a minority.

China needs the services of as many intellectuals as possible for the colossal task of socialist construction. We should trust the intellectuals who are really willing to serve the cause of socialism, and should radically improve our relations with them and help them solve any problems requiring solution, so that they can give full play to their talents. Many of our comrades are not good at uniting with intellectuals. They are too crude in dealing with them, lack respect for their work, and interfere in certain matters in scientific and cultural work where interference is unwarranted. We must do away with all such shortcomings.

The mass of intellectuals have made some progress, but they should not be complacent. They must continue to remould themselves, gradually shed their bourgeois world outlook and acquire the proletarian, communist world outlook so that they can fully fit in with the needs of the new society and unite with the workers and peasants. This change in world outlook is something fundamental, and up till now most of our intellectuals cannot be said to have accomplished it. We hope that they will continue to make progress and that, in the course of work and study, they will gradually acquire the communist world outlook, get a better grasp of Marxism-Leninism and become integrated with the workers and peasants. We hope they will not stop halfway, or, what is worse, slip back, for there will be no future for them in going backwards. Since our country's social system has changed and the economic base of bourgeois ideology has in the main been destroyed, not only is it necessary for large numbers of our intellectuals to change their world outlook, but they also have the possibility of doing so. But a thorough change in world outlook takes a very long time, and we should work patiently and not be impetuous. Actually, there are bound to be some who will always be ideologically reluctant to accept Marxism-Leninism and communism. We should not be too exacting in what we expect of them; as long as they comply with the requirements of the state and engage in legitimate pursuits, we should give them opportunities for suitable work.

Recently there has been a falling off in ideological and political work among students and intellectuals, and some unhealthy tendencies have appeared. Some people seem to think that there is no longer any need to concern oneself with politics or with the future of the motherland and the ideals of mankind. It seems as if Marxism was once all the rage but is currently not so much in fashion. To counter these tendencies, we must strengthen our ideological and political work. Both students and intellectuals should study hard. In addition to the study of their specialized subjects, they must make progress both ideologically and politically, which means that they should study Marxism, current events and political problems. Not to have a correct political point of view is like having no soul. The ideological remoulding carried on in the past was necessary and has yielded positive results. But it was carried on in a somewhat rough and ready fashion and the feelings of some people were hurt — this was not good. We must avoid such short-comings in future. All departments and organizations should shoulder their responsibilities in ideological and political work. This applies to the Communist Party, the Youth League, government departments in charge of this work, and especially to heads of educational institutions and teachers. Our educational policy must enable everyone who receives an education to develop morally, intellectually and physically and become a well-educated worker imbued with socialist consciousness. We must spread the idea of building our country through industriousness and thrift. We must help all our young people to understand that ours is still a very poor country, that we cannot change this situation radically in a short time, and that only through the united efforts of our younger generation and all our people, working with their own hands, can China be made strong and prosperous within a period of several decades. The establishment of our socialist system has opened the road leading to the ideal society of the future, but to translate this ideal into reality needs hard work. Some of our young people think that everything ought to be perfect once a socialist society is established and that they should be able to enjoy a happy life ready-made, without working for it. This is unrealistic.

VI. THE QUESTION OF THE MINORITY NATIONALITIES

The minority nationalities in our country number more than thirty million people. Although they constitute only

6 per cent of the total population, they inhabit extensive regions which altogether comprise 50 to 60 per cent of China's total area. It is imperative to foster good relations between the Han people and the minority nationalities. The key to this question lies in overcoming Han chauvinism. At the same time, efforts should also be made to overcome local nationalism, wherever it exists among the minority nationalities. Both Han chauvinism and local nationalism are harmful to the unity of the nationalities; they represent a specific contradiction among the people which should be overcome. We have already done some work in this sphere. In most areas inhabited by the minority nationalities, there has been a big improvement in relations among the nationalities, but a number of problems remain to be solved. In some areas, both Han chauvinism and local nationalism still exist to a serious degree, and this demands full attention. As a result of the efforts of the people of all nationalities over the last few years, democratic reforms and socialist transformation have in the main been completed in most of the minority nationality areas. Democratic reforms have not yet been carried out in Tibet because conditions are not ripe for them. According to the seventeen-point agreement reached between the Central People's Government and the local government of Tibet, the reform of the social system must be carried out, but the timing can only be decided by the great majority of the people of Tibet and their leading public figures when they consider it practicable, and one should not be impatient. It has now been decided not to proceed with democratic reforms in Tibet during the period of the Second Five-Year Plan. Whether they will be proceeded with in the period of the Third Five-Year Plan can only be decided in the light of the situation at that time.[5]

VII. OVERALL PLANNING AND PROPER ARRANGEMENT

By overall planning we mean planning which takes into consideration the interests of the 600 million people of our country. In drawing up plans, handling affairs or thinking over problems, we must proceed from the fact that China has a population of 600 million people, and we must never forget this fact. Why do we make a point of this? Is it possible that there are people who are still unaware that we have a population of 600 million? Yes, everyone knows this, but when it comes to actual practice, some people forget all about it and act as though the fewer the people, the smaller the circle, the better. Those who have this "small circle" mentality resist the idea of bringing all positive factors into play, of uniting with everyone that can be united with, and of doing everything possible to turn negative factors into positive ones so as to serve the great cause of building a socialist society. I hope these people will take a wider view and really recognize that we have a population of 600 million, that this is an objective fact, and that it is an asset. Our large population is a good thing, but of course it also involves certain difficulties. Construction is going ahead vigorously on all fronts and very successfully too, but in the present transitional period of tremendous social change there are still many difficult problems. Progress and at the same time difficulties — this is a contradiction. However, not only should contradictions be resolved, but they definitely can be. Our guiding principle is overall planning and proper arrangement. Whatever the problem — whether it concerns food, natural calamities, employment, education, the intellectuals, the united front of all patriotic forces, the minority nationalities, or anything else — we must always proceed from the standpoint of overall planning which takes the whole people into consideration and must make proper arrangements, after consultation with all circles concerned, in the light of the specific possibilities of the particular time and place. On no account should we complain that there are too many people, that they are backward, that things are troublesome and hard to handle, and so shut the problems out. Does this mean that the government alone must take care of everyone and everything? Of course not. In many cases, they can be left to the care of the public organizations or of the masses directly — both are quite capable of devising many good ways of handling things. This also comes within the scope of the principle of overall planning and proper arrangement. We should give guidance to the public organizations and the masses of the people everywhere in this respect.

VIII. ON "LET A HUNDRED FLOWERS BLOSSOM, LET A HUNDRED SCHOOLS OF THOUGHT CONTEND" AND "LONG-TERM COEXIST-ENCE AND MUTUAL SUPERVISION"

"Let a hundred flowers blossom, let a hundred schools of thought contend" and "long-term coexistence and mutual supervision" — how did these slogans come to be put forward? They were put forward in the light of China's specific conditions, on the basis of the recognition that various kinds of contradictions still exist in socialist society, and in response to the country's urgent need to speed up its economic and cultural development. Letting a hundred flowers blossom and a hundred schools of thought contend is the policy for promoting the progress of the arts and the sciences and a flourishing socialist culture in our land. Different forms and styles in art should develop freely and different schools in science should contend freely. We think that it is harmful to the growth of art and science if administrative measures are used to impose one particular style of art or school of thought and to ban another. Questions of right and wrong in the arts and sciences should be settled through free discussion in artistic and scientific circles and through practical work in these fields. They should not be settled in summary fashion. A period of trial is often needed to determine whether something is right or wrong. Throughout history, new and correct things have often failed at the outset to win recognition from the majority of people and have had to develop by twists and turns in struggle. Often correct and good things have first been regarded not as fragrant flowers but as poisonous weeds. Copernicus' theory of the solar system and Darwin's theory of evolution were once dismissed as erroneous and had to win through over bitter opposition. Chinese history offers many similar examples. In a socialist society, conditions for the growth of the new are radically different from and far superior to those in the old society. Nevertheless, it still often happens that new, rising forces are held back and rational proposals constricted. Moreover, the growth of new things may be hindered in the absence of deliberate suppression simply through lack of discernment. It is therefore necessary to be careful about questions of right and wrong in the arts and sciences, to encourage free discussion and avoid hasty conclusions. We believe that such an attitude can help to ensure a relatively smooth development of the arts and sciences.

Marxism, too, has developed through struggle. At the beginning, Marxism was subjected to all kinds of attack and regarded as a poisonous weed. It is still being attacked and is still regarded as a poisonous weed in many parts of the world. In the socialist countries, it enjoys a different position. But non-Marxist and, moreover, anti-Marxist ideologies exist even in these countries. In China, although in the main socialist transformation has been completed with respect to the system of ownership, and although the large-scale and turbulent class struggles of the masses characteristic of the previous revolutionary periods have in the main come to an end, there are still remnants of the overthrown landlord and comprador classes, there is still a bourgeoisie, and the remoulding of the petty bourgeoisie has only just started. The class struggle is by no means over. The class struggle between the proletariat and the bourgeoisie, the class struggle between the different political forces, and the class struggle in the ideological field between the proletariat and the bourgeoisie will continue to be long and tortuous and at times will even become very acute. The proletariat seeks to transform the world according to its own world outlook, and so does the bourgeoisie. In this respect, the question of which will win out, socialism or capitalism, is still not really settled. Marxists are still a minority among the entire population as well as among the intellectuals. Therefore, Marxism must still develop through struggle. Marxism can develop only through struggle, and not only is this true of the past and the present, it is necessarily true of the future as well. What is correct invariably develops in the course of struggle with what is wrong. The true, the good and the beautiful always exist by contrast with the false, the evil and the ugly, and grow in struggle with the latter. As soon as a wrong thing is rejected and a particular truth accepted by mankind, new truths begin their struggle with new errors. Such struggles will never end. This is the law of development of truth and, naturally, of Marxism as well.

It will take a fairly long period of time to decide the issue in the ideological struggle between socialism and capitalism in our country. The reason is that the influence of the bourgeoisie and of the intellectuals who come from the old society will remain in our country for a long time to come, and so will their class ideology. If this is not understood, or is not sufficiently understood, the gravest mistakes will be made and the necessity of waging the struggle in the ideological field will be ignored. Ideological struggle is not like other forms of struggle. The only method to be used in this struggle is that of painstaking reasoning and not crude coercion. Today, socialism is in an advantageous position in the ideological struggle. The main power of the state is in the hands of the working people led by the proletariat. The Communist Party is strong and its prestige stands high. Although there are defects and mistakes in our work, every fair-minded person can see that we are loyal to the people, that we are both determined and able to build up our motherland together with them, and that we have already achieved great successes and will achieve still greater ones. The vast majority of the bourgeoisie and intellectuals who come from the old society are patriotic and are willing to serve their flourishing socialist motherland; they know they will be helpless and have no bright future to look forward to if they turn away from the socialist cause and from the working people led by the Communist Party.

People may ask, since Marxism is accepted as the guiding ideology by the majority of the people in our country, can it be criticized? Certainly it can. Marxism is scientific truth and fears no criticism. If it did, and if it could be overthrown by criticism, it would be worthless. In fact, aren't the idealists criticizing Marxism every day and in every way? Aren't those who harbour bourgeois and petty-bourgeois ideas and do not wish to change — aren't they also criticizing Marxism in every way? Marxists should not be afraid of criticism from any quarter. Quite the contrary, they need to temper and develop themselves and win new positions in the teeth of criticism and in the storm and stress of struggle. Fighting against wrong ideas is like being vaccinated — a man develops greater immunity from disease as a result of vaccination. Plants raised in hot-houses are unlikely to be sturdy. Carrying out the policy of letting a hundred flowers blossom and a hundred schools of thought contend will not weaken but strengthen the leading position of Marxism in the ideological field.

What should our policy be towards non-Marxist ideas? As far as unmistakable counter-revolutionaries and saboteurs of the socialist cause are concerned, the matter is easy: we simply deprive them of their freedom of speech. But incorrect ideas among the people are quite a different matter. Will it do to ban such ideas and deny them any opportunity for expression? Certainly not. It is not only futile but very harmful to use summary methods in dealing with ideological questions among the people, with questions concerned with man's mental world. You may ban the expression of wrong ideas, but the ideas will still be there. On the other hand, if correct ideas are pampered in hot-houses without being exposed to the elements or immunized from disease, they will not win out against erroneous ones. Therefore, it is only by employing the method of discussion, criticism and reasoning that we can really foster correct ideas and overcome wrong ones, and that we can really settle issues.

Inevitably, the bourgeoisie and petty bourgeoisie will give expression to their own ideologies. Inevitably, they will stubbornly express themselves on political and ideological questions by every possible means. You cannot expect them to do otherwise. We should not use the method of suppression and prevent them from expressing themselves, but should allow them to do so and at the same time argue with them and direct appropriate criticism at them. We must undoubtedly criticize wrong ideas of every description. It certainly would not be right to refrain from criticism, look on while wrong ideas spread unchecked and allow them to monopolize the field. Mistakes must be criticized and poisonous weeds fought wherever they crop up. However, such criticism should not be dogmatic, and the metaphysical method should not be used, but efforts should be made to apply the dialectical method. What is needed is scientific analysis and convincing argument. Dogmatic criticism settles nothing. We are against poisonous weeds of any kind, but we must carefully distinguish between what is really a poisonous weed and what is really a fragrant flower. Together with the masses of the people, we must learn to differentiate carefully between the two and to use correct methods to fight the poisonous weeds.

At the same time as we criticize dogmatism, we must direct our attention to criticizing revisionism. Revisionism, or Right opportunism, is a bourgeois trend of thought that is even more dangerous than dogmatism. The revisionists, the Right opportunists, pay lip-service to Marxism; they too attack "dogmatism". But what they are really attacking is the quintessence of Marxism. They oppose or distort materialism and dialectics, oppose or try to weaken the people's democratic dictatorship and the leading role of the Communist Party, and oppose or try to weaken socialist transformation and socialist construction. Even now, after the basic victory of the socialist revolution in our country, there are a number of people who vainly hope to restore the capitalist system and are fighting the working class on every front, including the ideological one. And their right-hand men in this struggle are the revisionists.

At first glance, the two slogans — let a hundred flowers blossom and let a hundred schools of thought contend — have no class character; the proletariat can turn them to account, and so can the bourgeoisie or other people. But different classes, strata and social groups each have their own views on what are fragrant flowers and what are poisonous weeds. What then, from the point of view of the broad masses of the people, should be the criteria today for distinguishing fragrant flowers from poisonous weeds? In the political life of our people, how should right be distinguished from wrong in one's words and actions? On the basis of the principles of our Constitution, the will of the overwhelming majority of our people and the common political positions which have been proclaimed on various occasions by our political parties and groups, we consider that, broadly speaking, the criteria should be as follows:

(1) Words and actions should help to unite, and not divide, the people of our various nationalities.

(2) They should be beneficial, and not harmful, to socialist transformation and socialist construction.

(3) They should help to consolidate, and not undermine or weaken, the people's democratic dictatorship.

(4) They should help to consolidate, and not undermine or weaken, democratic centralism.

(5) They should help to strengthen, and not discard or weaken, the leadership of the Communist Party.

(6) They should be beneficial, and not harmful, to international socialist unity and the unity of the peace-loving people of the world.

Of these six criteria, the most important are the socialist path and the leadership of the Party. These criteria are put forward not to hinder but to foster the free discussion of questions among the people. Those who disapprove of these criteria can still put forward their own views and argue their case. However, since the majority of the people have clear-cut criteria to go by, criticism and self-criticism can be conducted along proper lines, and the criteria can be applied to people's words and actions to determine whether they are right or wrong, whether they are fragrant flowers or poisonous weeds. These are political criteria. Naturally, in judging the validity of scientific theories or assessing the aesthetic value of works of art, additional pertinent criteria are needed. But these six political criteria are applicable to all activities in the arts and the sciences. In a socialist country like ours, can there possibly be any useful scientific or artistic activity which runs counter to these political criteria?

The views set out above are based on China's specific historical conditions. Conditions vary in different socialist countries and with different Communist Parties. Therefore, we do not maintain that other countries and Parties should or must follow the Chinese way.

The slogan "long-term coexistence and mutual supervision" is also a product of China's specific historical conditions. It was not put forward all of a sudden, but had been in the making for several years. The idea of long-term coexistence had been there for a long time. After the socialist system was basically established last year, the slogan was put forward in explicit terms. Why should the bourgeois and petty-bourgeois democratic parties be allowed to exist side by side with the party of the working class over a long period of time? Because we have no reason for not adopting the policy of long-term coexistence with all those political parties which are truly devoted to the task of uniting the people for the cause of socialism and which enjoy the trust of the people. As early as June 1950, at the Second Session of the National Committee of the People's Political Consultative Conference, I put the matter in this way:

> The people and the People's Government have no reason to reject anyone or to deny him the opportunity of making a living and rendering service to the country, provided he is really willing to serve the people, and provided he really helped the people when times were difficult, did good before and keeps on doing good without giving up halfway.

What I was discussing here was the political basis for the long-term coexistence of the various parties. It is the desire as well as the policy of the Communist Party to exist side by side with the various democratic parties for a long time to come. But whether these democratic parties can remain in existence for long depends not merely on the desire of the Communist Party but on how well they acquit themselves and on whether they enjoy the confidence of the people. Mutual supervision among the various parties is also a long-established fact, in the sense that they have long been advising and criticizing each other. Mutual supervision is obviously not a one-sided matter; it means that the Communist Party should exercise supervision over the democratic parties, and vice versa. Why should the democratic parties be allowed to exercise supervision over the Communist Party? Because a party as much as an individual has great need to hear opinions different from its own. We all know that supervision over the Communist Party is mainly exercised by the working people and the Party membership. But the existence of the democratic parties is also to our benefit. Of course, the advice and criticism exchanged by the Communist Party and the democratic parties will play a positive supervisory role only when they conform to the six political criteria given above. Thus, we hope that in order to fit in with the needs of the new society, all the democratic parties will pay attention to ideological remoulding and strive for long-term coexistence with the Communist Party and mutual supervision.

IX. ON THE QUESTION OF DISTURBANCES
CREATED BY SMALL NUMBERS OF PEOPLE

In 1956, small numbers of workers or students in certain places went on strike. The immediate cause of these disturbances was the failure to satisfy certain of their demands for material benefits, of which some should and could have been met, while others were out of place or excessive and therefore could not be met for the time being. But a more important cause was bureaucracy on the part of the leadership. In some cases, the responsibility for such bureaucratic mistakes falls on the higher authorities, and those at lower levels are not entirely to blame. Another cause of these disturbances was lack of ideological and political education among the workers and students. In the same year, some members of agricultural co-operatives also created disturbances, and here too the main causes were bureaucracy on the part of the leadership and lack of educational work among the masses.

It should be admitted that some people are prone to pay attention to immediate, partial and personal interests and do not understand, or do not sufficiently understand, long-range, national and collective interests. Because of their lack of experience in political and social life, quite a number of young people are unable to see the contrast between the old China and the new, and it is not easy for them thoroughly to comprehend the hardships our people went through in the struggle to free themselves from the oppression of the imperialists and Kuomintang reactionaries, or the long period of arduous work needed before a happy socialist society can be established. That is why we must constantly carry on lively and effective political education among the masses and should always tell them the truth about the difficulties that crop up and discuss with them how to surmount these difficulties.

We do not approve of disturbances, because contradictions among the people can be resolved in accordance with the formula of "unity, criticism, unity", while disturbances are bound to cause some losses and are not conducive to the advance of socialism. We believe that the masses of the people support socialism, consciously observe discipline and are reasonable, and will certainly not take part in disturbances without due cause. But this does not mean that there is no possibility of disturbances in our country. On this question, we should pay attention to the following:

(1) In order to root out the causes of disturbances, we must stamp out bureaucracy, greatly improve ideological and political education, and deal with all contradictions properly. If this is done, generally speaking there will be no more disturbances.

(2) If disturbances do occur as a result of bad work on our part, then we should guide those involved on to the correct path, make use of the disturbances as a special means for improving our work and educating the cadres and the masses, and work out solutions to those questions which were previously left unsolved. In handling any disturbance, we should work painstakingly and must not use over-simplified methods, or hastily declare the matter closed. The ringleaders in disturbances should not be summarily removed from their jobs or expelled, except for those who have committed criminal offences or are active counter-revolutionaries and have to be dealt with according to law. In a large country like ours, there is nothing to get alarmed about if small numbers of people create disturbances; on the contrary, such disturbances will help us get rid of bureaucracy.

There are also a small number of people in our society who, disregarding the public interest, wilfully break the law and commit crimes. They are apt to take advantage of our policies and distort them, deliberately put forward unreasonable demands in order to incite the masses, or deliberately spread rumours to create trouble and disrupt public order. We do not propose to let these people have their way. On the contrary, proper legal action must be taken against them. The punishment of such people is the demand of the masses, and it would run counter to the popular will if they were not punished.

X. CAN BAD THINGS BE TURNED INTO GOOD THINGS?

In our society, as I have said, it is bad when some people create disturbances, and we do not approve of it. But when disturbances do occur, they enable us to learn lessons, to overcome bureaucracy and to educate the cadres and the masses. In this sense, bad things can be turned into good things. Disturbances thus have a dual character. Every disturbance can be regarded in this way.

Everybody knows that the Hungarian events were not a good thing. But they too had a dual character. Because our Hungarian comrades took proper action in the course of the events, what was a bad thing has eventually turned into a good one. The Hungarian state is now more firmly established than ever, and all other countries in the socialist camp have also learned a lesson.

Similarly, the world-wide campaign against communism and the people launched in the latter half of 1956 was of course a bad thing. But it educated and tempered the Communist Parties and the working class in all countries, and thus it has turned into a good thing. In the storm and stress of this period, a number of people withdrew from the Communist Party in many countries. Withdrawal from the Party reduces its membership and is, of course, a bad thing. But there is a good side to it, too. Vacillating elements who are unwilling to carry on have withdrawn, but the great majority of staunch Party members are more firmly united for the struggle. Why isn't this a good thing?

To sum up, we must learn to look at problems all-sidedly, seeing the reverse as well as the obverse side of things. In given conditions, a bad thing can lead to good results and a good thing to bad results. More than two thousand years ago Lao Tzu said: "Good fortune lieth within bad, bad fortune lurketh within good."[6] When the Japanese strode into China, they called this a victory. Huge parts of China's territory were seized, and the Chinese called this a defeat. But China's defeat contained the seeds of victory, while Japan's victory contained the seeds of defeat. Has not history proved this true?

People all over the world are now discussing whether or not a third world war will break out. On this question, too, we must be mentally prepared and do some analysis. We stand firmly for peace and against war. But if the imperialists insist on unleashing another war, we should not be afraid of it. Our attitude on this question is the same as our attitude towards any disturbance: first, we are against it; second, we are not afraid of it. The First World War was followed by the birth of the Soviet Union with a population of 200 million. The Second World War was followed by the emergence of the socialist camp with a combined population of 900 million. If the imperialists insist on launching a third world war, it is certain that several hundred million more will turn to socialism, and then there will not be much room left on earth for the imperialists; it is also likely that the whole structure of imperialism will utterly collapse.

In given conditions, each of the two opposing aspects of a contradiction invariably transforms itself into its opposite as a result of the struggle between them. Here, the conditions are essential. Without the given conditions, neither of the two contradictory aspects can transform itself into its opposite. Of all the classes in the world the proletariat is the one which is most eager to change its position, and next comes the semi-proletariat, for the former possesses nothing at all while the latter is hardly better off. The present situation in which the United States controls a majority in the United Nations and dominates many parts of the world is a temporary one, which will eventually be changed. China's position as a poor country denied her rights in international affairs will also be changed — the poor country will change into a rich one, the country denied its rights into one enjoying its rights — a transformation of things into their opposites. Here, the decisive conditions are the socialist system and the concerted efforts of a united people.

XI. ON PRACTISING ECONOMY

Here I wish to speak briefly on practising economy. We want to carry on large-scale construction, but our country is still very poor — herein lies a contradiction. One way of resolving it is to make a sustained effort to practise strict economy in every field.

During the *san fan* (or three anti's) movement in 1952, we fought against corruption, waste and bureaucracy, with the emphasis on combating corruption. In 1955 we advocated the practice of economy with great success, our emphasis then being on combating the unduly high standards for nonproductive projects in capital construction, and on economy in the use of raw materials in industrial production. But at that time economy was not yet applied in earnest as a guiding principle in all branches of the national economy, or in government offices, army units, schools and people's organizations in general. This year we are calling for economy and the elimination of waste in every sphere throughout the country. We still lack experience in the work of construction. During the last few years, great successes have been achieved, but there has also been waste. We must build up a number of large-scale modern enterprises step by step to form the mainstay of our industry, without which we shall not be able to turn our country into a strong modern industrial power within the coming decades. But the majority of our enterprises should not be built on such a scale; we should set up more small and medium enterprises and make full use of the industrial base left over from the old society, so as to effect the greatest economy and do more with less money. Good results have begun to appear in the few months since the principle of practising strict economy and combating waste was put forward, in more emphatic terms than before, by the Second Plenary Session of the Central Committee of the Communist Party of China in November 1956. The present economy campaign must be conducted in a thorough and sustained way. Like the criticism of any other faults or mistakes, the fight against waste may be compared to washing one's face. Don't people wash their faces every day? The Chinese Communist Party, the democratic parties, the democrats with no party affiliation, the intellectuals, industrialists and merchants, workers, peasants and handicraftsmen — in short, all the 600 million people of our country — must strive for increased production and economy, and against extravagance and waste. This is of prime importance not only economically, but politically as well. A dangerous tendency has shown itself of late among many of our personnel — an unwillingness to share the joys and hardships of the masses, a concern for personal fame and gain. This is very bad. One way of overcoming it is to simplify our organizations in the course of our campaign to increase production and practise economy, and to transfer cadres to lower levels so that a considerable number will return to productive work. We must see to it that all our cadres and all our people constantly bear in mind that ours is a big socialist country but an economically backward and poor one, and that this is a very great contradiction. To make China rich and strong needs several decades of intense effort, which will include, among other things, the effort to practise strict economy and combat waste, *i.e.,* the policy of building up our country through hard work and thrift.

XII. CHINA'S PATH TO INDUSTRIALIZATION

In discussing our path to industrialization, I am here concerned principally with the relationship between the growth of heavy industry, light industry and agriculture. It must be affirmed that heavy industry is the core of China's economic construction. At the same time, full attention must be paid to the development of agriculture and light industry.

As China is a large agricultural country, with over 80 per cent of her population in the rural areas, industry must develop together with agriculture, for only thus can industry secure raw materials and a market, and only thus is it possible to accumulate fairly large funds for building a powerful heavy industry. Everyone knows that light industry is closely related to agriculture. Without agriculture there can be no light industry. But it is not yet so clearly understood that agriculture provides heavy industry with an important market. This fact, however, will be more readily appreciated as gradual progress in the technical improvement and modernization of agriculture calls for more and more machinery, fertilizer, water conservancy and electric power projects and transport facilities for the farms, as well as fuel and building materials for the rural consumers. During the period of the Second and Third Five-Year Plans, the entire national economy will benefit if we can achieve an even greater growth in our agriculture and thus induce a correspondingly greater development of light industry. As agriculture and light industry develop, heavy industry, assured of its market and funds, will grow faster. Hence what may seem to be a slower pace of industrialization will actually not be so slow, and indeed may even be faster. In three five-year plans or perhaps a little longer, China's annual steel output can be raised to 20,000,000 tons or more, as compared with the peak pre-liberation output of something over 900,000 tons in 1943. This will gladden the people both in the town and in the countryside.

I do not propose to dwell on economic questions today. With barely seven years of economic construction behind us, we still lack experience and need to accumulate it. We had no experience of revolution either when we first started, and it was only after we had taken a number of tumbles and acquired experience that we won nation-wide victory. What we must demand of ourselves now is to cut down the time needed for gaining experience of economic construction to a shorter period than it took us to gain experience of revolution, and not to pay as high a price for it. Some price we will have to pay, but we hope it will not be as high as that paid during the period of revolution. We must realize that there is a contradiction here — the contradiction between the objective laws of economic development of a socialist society and our subjective understanding of them — which needs to be resolved in the course of practice. This contradiction also manifests itself as a contradiction between different people, that is, a contradiction between those with a relatively accurate understanding of these objective laws and those with a relatively inaccurate understanding of them; this, too, is a contradiction among the people. Every contradiction is an objective reality, and it is our task to understand it and resolve it as correctly as we can.

In order to turn our country into an industrial power, we must learn conscientiously from the advanced experience of the Soviet Union. The Soviet Union has been building socialism for forty years, and its experience is very valuable to us. Let us ask: Who designed and equipped so many important factories for us? Was it the United States? Or Britain? No, neither of them. Only the Soviet Union was willing to do so, because it is a socialist country and our ally. In addition to the Soviet Union, some East European fraternal countries have also given us some assistance. It is perfectly true that we should learn from the good experience of all countries, socialist or capitalist, and there is no argument about this point. But the main thing is still to learn from the Soviet Union. Now, there are two different attitudes towards learning from others. One is the dogmatic attitude of transplanting everything, whether or not it is suited to our conditions. This is no good. The other attitude is to use our heads and learn those things which suit our conditions, that is, to absorb whatever experience is useful to us. That is the attitude we should adopt.

To strengthen our solidarity with the Soviet Union, to strengthen our solidarity with all the socialist countries — this is our fundamental policy, this is where our basic interest lies. Then there are the Asian and African countries and all the peace-loving countries and peoples — we must strengthen and develop our solidarity with them. United with these two forces, we shall not stand alone. As for the imperialist countries, we should unite with their peoples and strive to coexist peacefully with those countries, do business with them and prevent any possible war, but under no circumstances should we harbour any unrealistic notions about them.

NOTES

[1] The Hungarian events refer to the counter-revolutionary rebellion in Hungary in 1956. In late October of that year, counter-revolutionary disturbances instigated by the imperialists broke out in socialist Hungary; Communists and other revolutionaries were massacred *en masse* and Budapest, the capital, was seized for a time. The imperialists attempted in vain to make a breach in the socialist camp *via* Hungary, with the object of destroying the socialist countries one by one. On November 4, the Hungarian people established their revolutionary workers' and peasants' government and smashed the plot for a counter-revolutionary restoration, with the help of the Soviet army and the sympathy and support of the entire socialist camp and the progressive forces of the world.

[2] The payment of a fixed rate of interest to the national bourgeoisie in order to buy up their means of production in the course of socialist transformation is part of the policy of redemption adopted by the state. Since the conversion of capitalist industry and commerce trade by trade into joint state-private enterprises in 1956, the state has been paying the national bourgeoisie a fixed rate of interest on the money value of their assets, such payment to run for a given period of time. This interest is still a form of exploitation.

[3] In 1957, at the suggestion of Comrade Mao Tse-tung, the Central Government and the local governments at all levels made a comprehensive review of the work of suppressing counter-revolutionaries. The results showed that great successes had been achieved in the struggle against counter-revolutionaries; except for a few individual instances, nearly all cases had been handled correctly and, moreover, mistakes had been corrected whenever discovered. In the summer of 1957, however, taking advantage of our review of the work of suppressing counter-revolutionaries, the bourgeois Rightists stirred up trouble in an

attempt to negate our achievements in this field and attacked the Party's policy of suppressing counter-revolutionaries. Opposed by the people throughout the country, their schemes came to naught.

[4] The Wang Kuo-fan Co-operative was the Chien Ming Farming, Forestry and Animal Husbandry Producers' Co-operative in Hsiszushihlipu Village, Tsunhua County, Hopei Province. Under the leadership of its director Wang Kuo-fan, it became well known for its industriousness and thrift. In September 1958, the co-operative expanded into the Chien Ming People's Commune, with Wang Kuo-fan as the director.

[5] Democratic reforms were later introduced in Tibet ahead of the time mentioned. On March 19, 1959, the reactionaries in the local government and the upper social strata of Tibet launched a full-scale armed rebellion after long planning and preparation in collusion with imperialists and foreign interventionists. With active support from the masses of patriotic Tibetans, both lamas and laymen, the People's Liberation Army quickly put down the rebellion. Democratic reforms were then introduced throughout the vast area of Tibet, whose people were thus liberated from the darkest and most barbarous serfdom.

[6] See Lao Tzu, *Tao Te Ching*, Chapter 58.

WHERE DO CORRECT IDEAS COME FROM?

May 1963

Where do correct ideas come from? Do they drop from the skies? No. Are they innate in the mind? No. They come from social practice, and from it alone; they come from three kinds of social practice, the struggle for production, the class struggle and scientific experiment. It is man's social being that determines his thinking. Once the correct ideas characteristic of the advanced class are grasped by the masses, these ideas turn into a material force which changes society and changes the world. In their social practice, men engage in various kinds of struggle and gain rich experience, both from their successes and from their failures. Countless phenomena of the objective external world are reflected in a man's brain through his five sense organs — the organs of sight, hearing, smell, taste and touch. At first, knowledge is perceptual. The leap to conceptual knowledge, *i.e.*, to ideas, occurs when sufficient perceptual knowledge is accumulated. This is one process in cognition. It is the first stage in the whole process of cognition, the stage leading from objective

---

This passage is from the "Draft Decision of the Central Committee of the Chinese Communist Party on Certain Problems in Our Present Rural Work", which was drawn up under the direction of Comrade Mao Tse-tung. The passage was written by Comrade Mao Tse-tung himself.

matter to subjective consciousness, from existence to ideas. Whether or not one's consciousness or ideas (including theories, policies, plans or measures) do correctly reflect the laws of the objective external world is not yet proved at this stage, in which it is not yet possible to ascertain whether they are correct or not. Then comes the second stage in the process of cognition, the stage leading from consciousness back to matter, from ideas back to existence, in which the knowledge gained in the first stage is applied in social practice to ascertain whether the theories, policies, plans or measures meet with the anticipated success. Generally speaking, those that succeed are correct and those that fail are incorrect, and this is especially true of man's struggle with nature. In social struggle, the forces representing the advanced class sometimes suffer defeat not because their ideas are incorrect but because, in the balance of forces engaged in struggle, they are not as powerful for the time being as the forces of reaction; they are therefore temporarily defeated, but they are bound to triumph sooner or later. Man's knowledge makes another leap through the test of practice. This leap is more important than the previous one. For it is this leap alone that can prove the correctness or incorrectness of the first leap, *i.e.*, of the ideas, theories, policies, plans or measures formulated in the course of reflecting the objective external world. There is no other way of testing truth. Furthermore, the one and only purpose of the proletariat in knowing the world is to change it. Often, a correct idea can be arrived at only after many repetitions of the process leading from matter to consciousness and then back to matter, that is, leading from practice to knowledge and then back to practice. Such is the Marxist theory of knowledge, the dialectical materialist theory of knowledge.   Among our comrades there are many who do not yet understand this theory of knowledge. When asked the source of their ideas, opinions, policies, methods, plans and conclusions, eloquent speeches and long articles, they consider the question strange and cannot answer it.   Nor do they comprehend that matter can be transformed into consciousness and consciousness into matter, although such leaps are phenomena of everyday life.   It is therefore necessary to educate our comrades in the dialectical materialist theory of knowledge, so that they can orientate their thinking correctly, become good at investigation and study and at summing up experience, overcome difficulties, commit fewer mistakes, do their work better, and struggle hard so as to build China into a great and powerful socialist country and help the broad masses of the oppressed and exploited throughout the world in fulfilment of our great internationalist duty.